Children of the Mire   *The Charles Eliot Norton Lectures, 1971-1972*

Children of the Mire

Modern Poetry from Romanticism to the Avant-Garde

New and Enlarged Edition

OCTAVIO PAZ   Translated by Rachel Phillips

Harvard University Press
Cambridge, Massachusetts, and London, England
1991

Library of Congress Cataloging-in-Publication Data

Paz, Octavio. 1914–
  Children of the mire : modern poetry from Romanticism to the avant-
garde / Octavio Paz ; translated by Rachel Phillips. — New and enl. ed.
    p.   cm. — (The Charles Eliot Norton lectures ; 1971–1972)
  Includes bibliographical references.
  ISBN 0-674-11629-1 (pbk.)
    1. Poetry, Modern—History and criticism.   I. Title.   II. Series.
PN1161.P3   1991   90-26837
809.1′03—dc20   CIP

Preface

In *El arco y la lira* (Mexico, 1956), published many years ago,
I tried to answer three questions about poetry. What is a poem?
What do poems say? How do poems communicate? This book is
an amplification of the response I tried to make to the third of
these questions. A poem is an object fashioned out of the
language, rhythms, beliefs, and obsessions of a poet and a
society. It is the product of a definite history and a definite
society, but its historical mode of existence is contradictory.
The poem is a device which produces anti-history, even though
this may not be the poet's intention. The poetic process inverts
and converts the passage of time; the poem does not stop time —
it contradicts and transfigures it. Whether we are talking about
a baroque sonnet, a popular epic, or a fable, within its confines
time passes differently from time in history or in what we call
real life. Contradiction between history and poetry is found in
all societies, but only in the modern age is it so manifest.
Response to and awareness of the discord between society and
poetry has been the central, often secret, theme of poetry since
the Romantic era. In this book I have tried to describe, from
the perspective of a Spanish American poet, the modern poetic
movement and its contradictory relationships with what we
call "the modern."

Despite language and cultural differences the Western world has only one modern poetry. It is hardly necessary to point out that "Western" embraces Anglo-American and Latin American poetic traditions (the latter with three branches: Spanish, Portuguese, and French). To illustrate the unity of modern poetry I have chosen those episodes of its history which I consider most relevant: its birth in English and German Romanticism; its metamorphosis into French Symbolism and Spanish American *modernismo*; and, finally, its culmination in the avant-garde trends of the twentieth century. From its earliest days modern poetry has been a reaction against the modern era, tugging first in one direction then another as the manifestations of the modern have changed—the Enlightenment, critical reason, liberalism, positivism, and Marxism. This explains the ambiguity of its relationships—almost always beginning with an enthusiastic devotion followed by a brusque rupture—with the revolutionary movements of the modern age, from the French Revolution to the Russian. In their opposition to modern rationalism poets rediscover a tradition, as ancient as man, which was kept alive by Renaissance Neoplatonism and the hermetic and occultist sects and tendencies of the sixteenth and seventeenth centuries. This tradition crosses the eighteenth century, penetrates the nineteenth, and reaches our own. I am referring to analogy, the vision of the universe as a system of correspondences, and of language as the universe's double.

Analogy as the Romantics and Symbolists understood it is subverted by irony, that is to say, by the consciousness of the modern age and its criticism of Christianity and other religions. The twentieth century turns irony into humor—black, green, or purple. Analogy and irony confront the poet with the rationalism and progressivism of the modern age; at the same time and just as violently they put him face to face with Christianity. Modern poetry's theme is twofold: it is a contradictory dialogue with and against modern revolutions and the Christian faiths; and within poetry and each poetic work, there is a dialogue between analogy and irony. The context within which this double dialogue unfolds is yet another dialogue: modern poetry can be seen as the history of contradictory relationships, fascination and repulsion intertwined, between Romance and Germanic languages, the central tradition of Greco-Latin Classicism and the eccentric tradition of the individual and the bizarre represented by Romanticism; syllabic and accentual verse.

Avant-garde movements in the twentieth century trace the same patterns as in the previous century, but in inverse direction. The "modernism" of the Anglo-American poets is an attempt to return to the central tradition of Europe—the exact opposite of German and English Romanticism—while French Surrealism carries German Romanticism to its furthest extreme. Our own period marks the end of the avant-garde, and thereby of everything which since the eighteenth century has been called *modern art*. What is in question in the second half of our century is not the idea of art itself, but the idea of the modern. At the end of this book I deal with poetry that has come into existence since the avant-garde. Those pages unite with *Los signos en rotación*, a poetic manifesto I published in 1965, which now serves as the epilogue to *El arco y la lira*.

I wish to acknowledge my gratitude to the translator, Rachel

Phillips, to Ann Louise McLaughlin, and to the poet William Ferguson, who helped me revise the lectures (the Charles Eliot Norton Lectures) which make up this book.

O. P.

Contents

1 A Tradition against Itself   1

2 The Revolt of the Future   19

3 Children of the Mire   38

4 Analogy and Irony   58

5 Translation and Metaphor   78

6 The Closing of the Circle   102

   Revolution/Eros/Meta-Irony   103
   The Pattern Reversed   115
   The Twilight of the Avant-Garde   162

   Notes   178

   Sources and Credits   190

Mais l'oracle invoqué pour jamais dut se taire;
Un seul pouvait au monde expliquer ce mystère:
—Celui qui donna l'âme aux enfants du limon.

Gérard de Nerval
(*Le Christ aux Oliviers*, V)

1 A Tradition against Itself

The title of this chapter, "A Tradition against Itself," at first
seems a contradiction. Can "tradition" be that which severs the
chain and interrupts the continuity? Could this negation
become a tradition without denying itself? The tradition of
discontinuity implies the negation not only of tradition but of
discontinuity as well. Nor is the contradiction resolved by
replacing the phrase "a tradition against itself" with words less
obviously contradictory—such as "the Modern Tradition." How
can the modern be traditional?

Despite the implicit contradiction—sometimes with full
awareness of it, as Baudelaire's reflections in *L'art romantique*—
since the beginning of the last century modernity has been
termed a tradition, and rejection considered the privileged form
of change. To say that modernity is a tradition is slightly
inaccurate; I should say the *other* tradition. Modernity is a
polemical tradition which displaces the tradition of the moment,
whatever it happens to be, but an instant later yields its place to
still another tradition which in turn is a momentary manifestation of modernity. Modernity is never itself; it is always *the
other*. The modern is characterized not only by novelty but by
otherness. A bizarre tradition and a tradition of the bizarre,

> polemic – a controversy or refutation
> polemics – art or practice of debate

modernity is condemned to pluralism: the old tradition was always the same, the modern is always different. The former postulates unity between past and present; the latter, not content with emphasizing its own differences, affirms that the past is not one but many. The tradition of the modern is thus radical otherness and plurality of pasts. The present will not tolerate the past; today will not be yesterday's child. What is modern breaks with the past, denies it entirely. Modernity is sufficient unto itself; it founds its own tradition. An example is the title of Harold Rosenberg's book on art, *The Tradition of the New*. Although the new may not be exactly the modern—certain novelties are not modern—this title expresses clearly and succinctly the paradox at the root of the art and poetry of our time, the intellectual principle simultaneously justifying and denying them, their nourishment and their poison. The art and poetry of our time live on modernity—and die from it.

In the history of Western poetry the cult of the new and the love of novelty appear with a regularity which I dare not call cyclical, but which is not random either. There are periods when the rule is the "imitation of the Ancients," others which glorify novelty and surprise. The English "metaphysical" and the Spanish Baroque poets are examples of the latter. Both practiced with equal enthusiasm the aesthetics of surprise. Novelty and surprise are kindred terms, but they are not the same. The conceits, metaphors, and other verbal devices of the Baroque poem are designed to amaze: what is new is new if it is unexpected. But seventeenth-century novelty was not critical nor did it imply the negation of tradition. On the contrary, it affirmed its continuity. Gracián says the Moderns

are more witty than the Ancients—not that they are different.
He enthuses over the works of certain of his contemporaries,
not because their authors have abandoned an older style,
but because they provide new and surprising combinations of
the same elements. Neither Góngora nor Gracián was revolutionary in the sense in which we use the word today; they did
not set out to change the ideas of beauty of their time—although
Góngora actually did. For them novelty was synonymous not
with change but with amazement. To find this strange marriage
of the aesthetics of surprise and negation, we must move to
the end of the eighteenth century, to the beginning of the
modern era. Since its birth, modernity has been a critical passion; insofar as it is both criticism and passion, it is a double
negation, as much of Classical geometries as of Baroque laby-
rinths. A dizzy passion, for its culmination is the negation of
itself; modernity is a sort of creative self-destruction. Since
Romanticism the poetic imagination has been building monuments on ground undermined by criticism. And it goes on doing
so, fully aware that it is undermined.

What distinguishes our modernity from that of other ages is
not our cult of the new and surprising, important though it is,
but the fact that it is a rejection, a criticism of the immediate
past, an interruption of continuity. Modern art is not only
the offspring of the age of criticism, it is also its own critic. The
new is not exactly the modern, unless it carries a double
explosive charge: the negation of the past and the affirmation
of something different. That "something" has changed name
and shape in the course of the last two centuries—from the
sensibility of the pre-Romantics to the meta-irony of Duchamp—

but it has always been that which is different, apart from and foreign to the reigning tradition, a singularity which bursts into the present and twists its course in an unexpected direction. It is controversial oddness, active opposition. We are seduced by the new not because of its newness but because of its differentness. This differentness is negation—the knife which splits time in two: before and now.

The very old can be adopted by modernity if it rejects the tradition of the moment and proposes a different one. Consecrated by the same controversial forces as the new, what is very old is not a past but a beginning. Our passion for contradictions resuscitates it, breathes life into it, and makes it our contemporary. Modern art and literature consist of continuous discovering of the very old and distant, from the popular Germanic poetry uncovered by Herder to the Chinese poetry recreated by Pound, from the Orient of Delacroix to the art of the South Seas so loved by Breton. The appearance of all these paintings, sculptures, and poems on our aesthetic horizon marked a break, a change. These hundred- and thousand-year-old novelties interrupted tradition time and time again; the history of modern art is linked with the resurrection of the art forms of vanished civilizations. As manifestations of the aesthetics of surprise, but even more as momentary incarnations of critical negation, the products of archaic art and of distant civilizations fit naturally into the tradition of discontinuity. They are among the masks of modernity.

The modern tradition erases dichotomies between the ancient and the contemporary and between the far-distant and the near-to-hand. The acid dissolving these differences is criticism.

Critical passion: excessive, impassioned love of criticism and its precise devices for disconstructions, but also criticism in love with its object, infatuated with the very thing it denies. In love with itself and at war with itself, it cannot affirm anything permanent or take any principle as a base, its sole principle being the negation of all principles, perpetual change. The meaning of this cult will escape us unless we are aware that it is rooted in a peculiar conception of time. For the Ancients, today repeats yesterday; for the Moderns, denies it. In the first case, time is seen and felt as a regulating factor, a process in which the variations and exceptions are actually variations from and exceptions to the rule; in the second, the process is a fabric of irregularities because variations and exceptions are themselves the rule. For us time does not repeat identical moments or centuries; each century and each instant is unique, different, *other*.

The tradition of the modern conceals a paradox greater than is hinted at in the contradiction between ancient and new, modern and traditional. The opposition between the past and the present vanishes because time passes so quickly that the distinctions among past, present, and future evaporate. We can speak of a modern tradition without contradicting ourselves because the modern era has eroded, almost to the point of disappearance, the antagonism between the old and the actual, the new and the traditional. The acceleration of time not only blurs the division between what has happened and what is happening but also eradicates the differences between old age and youth. Our era has exalted youth and its values with such frenzy as to make of this cult a superstition, if not a religion.

Yet never before has age overtaken us as rapidly as today.
Our art collections, our poetry anthologies, and our libraries
are full of prematurely aged styles, movements, paintings,
sculptures, novels, poems. We feel dizzy: what has just happened
already belongs to the world of the infinitely remote, while at
the same time the ancient of ancients is infinitely near. We
may conclude that the modern tradition and the contradictory
ideas and images evoked by this notion are the result of an
even more disturbing phenomenon: the modern era marks the
acceleration of historical time. If years, months, and days
actually do not pass more quickly now, at least more things
happen in them. And more things happen at the same time—not
in succession, but simultaneously. Such acceleration produces
fusion: all times and all spaces flow together in one here and
now.

Some may wonder if history really passes more quickly now
than before. Who can answer this question? The acceleration of
historic time might be an illusion; the changes and convulsions
that distress or fill us with wonder may be far less profound
and decisive than we think. The Russian Revolution seemed so
radical a break between past and future that a traveler said:
I have seen the future and it works. Today we are surprised by
the persistence of old Russia's traditional features. John Reed's
book recounting the electrifying days of 1917 seems to describe a far-distant past; that of the Marquis of Coustine, whose
theme is the bureaucratic and police-ridden world of Czarism, is
up-to-date in more ways than one. The Mexican Revolution
also impells us to doubt history's acceleration. It was a profound
upheaval, whose object was to modernize the country; yet the

most remarkable fact about contemporary Mexico is the persistence of ways of thinking and feeling that belong to the colonial
era, or even the pre-Hispanic world. The same is true of art
and literature. During the last century and a half there have
been many changes and aesthetic revolutions, but one and the
same principle inspired the German and English Romantics,
the French Symbolists, and the cosmopolitan vanguard of the
first half of the twentieth century. On various occasions
Frederick Schlegel defined romantic poetry, love, and irony
in terms not very different from those which, a century later,
André Breton used in speaking about the eroticism, imagination,
and humor of the Surrealists. Influences? Coincidences?
Neither: merely the persistence of certain ways of thinking,
seeing, and feeling.

Doubts about the reality of "the acceleration of history" grow
stronger if, instead of turning to the recent past for examples,
we compare distant ages or different civilizations. Georges
Dumézil has shown the existence of an ideology common to all
Indo-European peoples, from India and Iran to the Celtic and
Germanic worlds, an ideology which resisted and still resists
the double erosion of geographic and historical isolation.
Separated by thousands of miles and by thousands of years,
the Indo-Europeans still preserve the remains of a tripartite
conception of the world. I am convinced that something similar
is true of the Mongolian peoples, in Asia as well as in America;
that world is waiting for a Dumézil to show its profound unity.
Even before Benjamin Lee Whorf, who was the first to formu-
late systematically the contrast between the mental structures
underlying the Europeans and those of the Hopi, some

researchers had noticed the existence and the persistence of a quadripartite vision of the world common to the American Indians. But the differences between civilizations hide a secret unity: man. Cultural and historic differences are the work of a single author who changes very little. Human nature is no illusion: it is the constant factor that produces the changes and the diversity of cultures, histories, religions, arts.

We might conclude that the acceleration of history is illusory or, more probably, that the changes merely touch the surface without altering the deep reality. Events follow each other and the swell of history conceals the underwater landscape of motionless valleys and mountains. In what sense, then, can we talk of a modern tradition? The acceleration of history may be illusory or real—the point legitimately can be questioned—but the society which invented the expression "the modern tradition" is a peculiar one. The phrase implies more than a logical and linguistic contradiction: it expresses that dramatic condition of our civilization which seeks its foundation not in the past or in some immovable principle, but in change. Whether we believe that social structures change very slowly and mental structures are invariable, or whether we believe in history and its unending transformations, one fact remains: our image of time has changed. The comparison of our idea of time with that of a twelfth-century Christian makes the difference immediately apparent.

As our image of time has changed, so has our relation to tradition. Criticism of a tradition begins with the awareness of belonging to a tradition. Traditionalist peoples live immersed in their past without questioning it. Unaware of their traditions, they live with and in them. Once a man realizes that he belongs to a tradition, he knows implicitly that he is different from that tradition; sooner or later this knowledge impels him to question, examine, and sometimes deny it. Our age is distinguished from other epochs and other societies by the image we have made of time. For us time is the substance of history, time unfolds in history. The meaning of "the modern tradition" emerges more clearly: it is an expression of our historic consciousness. It is a criticism of the past, and it is an attempt, repeated several times throughout the last two centuries, to found a tradition on the only principle immune to criticism, because it is the condition and the consequence of criticism: change, history.

The relation between past, present, and future differs in each civilization. In primitive societies the temporal archetype, model for the present and future, is the past—not the recent past, but an immemorial past lying beyond all pasts, at the beginning of the beginning. Like a wellspring, this past of pasts flows constantly, runs into and becomes part of the present; it is the only actuality which really counts. Social life is not historic but ritualistic; it is made up not of a succession of changes but of the rhythmic repetition of the timeless past. Always present, this past protects society from change by serving as a model for imitation and by being periodically actualized in ritual. The past has a double nature: it is an immutable time, impervious to change; it is not what happened once, but what always happens. The past escapes both accident and contingency; although it is time, it is also the negation of time. It dissolves the contradictions between what happened yesterday and what is happening today. Insensible to change, it is the norm: everything must happen as in the timeless past.

Nothing could be more opposed to our conception of time than that of the primitives; for us time is the bearer of change, for them the agent suppressing it. More than a category of time, the past of primitive man is a reality beyond time: the original beginning. All societies except ours have imagined a place beyond, where time reposes reconciled with itself. It no longer changes because, having become immobile transparency, it has ceased to flow, or because, flowing endlessly, it remains identical to itself. The principle of identity triumphs: contradictions disappear because perfect time exists outside time. For primitive peoples, as opposed to Christians or Muslims, the atemporal model exists not afterward but before, not at the end of time but at the beginning of the beginning. It is not the state at which we must arrive when time is abolished, but what we must imitate from the beginning.

Primitive society views with dread the variations implied by the passage of time; changes are considered ominous. What we call history is a fault, a fall. Oriental and Mediterranean civilizations, like those of pre-Columbian America, regarded history with the same misgivings, but did not deny it so radically. The past of the primitives is always motionless and always present; the time of Oriental and Mediterranean cultures unfolds in circles and in spirals: the ages of the world. A surprising transformation of the timeless past, it elapses, is subject to change, becomes temporal. The past is the primordial seed sprouting, growing, exhausting itself, and dying—to be born again. The model is still the past before all eras, the happy time of the beginning, governed by the harmony of heaven and earth. But it is a past which possesses the same properties as plants and living beings; it is an animated substance, that changes, and, above all, dies. History is a debasement of original time, a slow, inexorable process of decadence ending in death. Recurrence is the remedy for change and extinction; the past waits at the end of each cycle. The past is an age to come. The future offers a double image: the end of time and its rebirth, the corruption of the archetypal past and its resurrection. The end of the cycle is the restoration of the original past—and the beginning of the inevitable downfall. This conception differs markedly from those of the Christians and the moderns. For the Christians, perfect time is eternity—time abolished, history annulled; for the moderns, perfection, if it exists, can be found only in the future. Also, our future resembles neither the past nor the present; it is the region of the unexpected, whereas the future of the ancient Mediterraneans and Orientals runs into the past.

The Western World has a name for this primordial time which is the model of all times, the age of harmony between man and nature and between man and men: the Golden Age. In other civilizations—the Chinese, the Meso-American—jade, not gold, symbolized the harmony between the social scheme of humans and that of nature. Jade embodies the ever-returning green of nature, just as gold bears witness to a materialization of the light of the sun. Jade and gold are double symbols, like everything which expresses the deaths and resurrections of cyclical time. In one phase time is condensed and transmuted into a hard, precious substance, as if it wished to escape from change and its debasement; in the other, stone and metal become soft, are again time, and, turned into vegetable and animal excrement and rottenness, disintegrate. But disintegration and putrefaction are also resurrection and fertility: the ancient Mexicans put a jade bead on the mouths of their dead.

The ambiguity of gold and jade reflects the ambiguity of cyclical time: the temporal archetype exists in time and adopts the form of a past which returns—only to move away again. Green or golden, the happy time is a time of concord, a conjunction of times, lasting only a moment. It is a true accord: the condensation of time in a drop of jade or gold is followed by dispersion and corruption. Recurrence saves us from the changes of history only to submit us to them more harshly. They cease to be accident, fall, or error, and become the successive moments of an inexorable process. Nor do the gods escape the cycle. From the Egyptians and the Greeks to the Aztecs, all mythologies tell the story of the birth, death, and resurrection of the gods. In a Nahuatl poem Quetzalcoatl disappears on the horizon, "where the waters of the sea meet those of the heavens." He will reappear on the same horizon, where twilight becomes dawn.

Is there no way to step out of the circle of time? From the beginning of her civilization, India imagined a beyond which is not properly time but its negation: motionless being identical to itself (Brahman) or an equally motionless vacuity (Nirvana). Brahman never changes, and nothing can be said about it, except that it is; about Nirvana nothing can be said, not even that it is not. In both cases we are dealing with a reality beyond time and language, a reality admitting of no names other than those of universal negation, for it is neither this nor that, nor what lies beyond. It is neither this nor that, and yet it is. Indian civilization does not break cyclical time; without denying its empirical reality, it dissolves and converts it into an insubstantial phantasmagoria. This criticism of time, which reduces change to an illusion, is another, more radical way, of opposing history. The timeless past of primitive man becomes temporal, is made incarnate, and becomes the cyclical time of the Mediterranean and Eastern civilizations; India dissolves cycles: they are literally the dream of Brahman. Each time the god wakes, the dream dissolves. The duration of this dream terrifies me; the age in which we now live—rather the dream of this age, characterized by the unjust possession of wealth—will last four hundred and thirty-two thousand years. And it appalls me even more to know that every time the god awakens he is condemned to fall asleep again and to dream the same dream. This vast, circular dream, at once monstrous and monotonous, is unreal for him who dreams it but real for us who are dreamt. The danger of this metaphysical radicalism is that man cannot escape the universal negation. Between history with its unreal cycles and a colorless reality devoid of flavor and attributes, what remains for man? Both are uninhabitable (see Note 1).

India dispelled cycles; Christianity severed them. Before the moment of illumination Gautama recalls his past lives and sees, in other universes and other cosmic eras, other Gautamas disappearing in vacuity. Christ came to earth only once. The world in which Christianity propagated itself was haunted by a belief in its inevitable decadence, and men were convinced they were living the end of a cycle. At times this idea was expressed in almost Christian terms: "The earthly elements will be dissolved and all will be destroyed so that all may be created anew in its first innocence." The first part of this sentence by Seneca corresponds to what the Christians believed and hoped, that the end of the world was near. It is very possible that one of the reasons for the great number of conversions to the new religion was the belief in the imminence of the end. Christianity offered an answer to the threat which loomed over mankind. Would so many have been converted if they had known that the world would last several millenniums more? Saint Augustine thought that the first age of humanity, from the Fall of Adam to the sacrifice of Christ, had lasted a little less than six thousand years, and that the last age, ours, would endure only a few centuries. The circular time of the pagan philosophers implied the return of a golden age, but this universal regeneration, apart from being only a respite in the inexorable movement toward decadence, was not synonymous with individual salvation. Christianity promised personal salvation, so its triumph produced an essential change: the protagonist of the cosmic drama was no longer the world but man—or, rather, Everyman. History's center of gravity changed. The circular time of the pagans was infinite and impersonal; Christian time was finite and personal.

Augustine refutes the idea of cycles with curious arguments. He thinks it absurd that rational souls do not remember having lived all those lives of which the pagan philosophers spoke; and he thinks it even more absurd to postulate at one time wisdom and the eternal return: "How can the immortal soul

which has gained wisdom be submitted to these ceaseless migra-
tions between an illusory beatitude and a real unhappiness?"
The image of circular time becomes a demoniacal design, and
centuries later will make Raimundo Lull say "Grief in hell
is like the movement of the circle." Finite and personal,
Christian time is irreversible. It is not true, says Saint Augustine,
that for countless cycles Plato is condemned to teach, in a
school in Athens called the Academy, the same doctrines to the
same pupils: "Only once did Christ die for our sins, and rise
from the dead, and he will die no more." When it broke the
cycles and introduced the idea of a finite and irreversible time,
Christianity accentuated the "otherness" of time; it made
manifest that property which makes time break with itself,
divide and separate itself, become something other and always
different. Adam's Fall severed the eternal present of Paradise:
the beginning of sequential time is the beginning of separation.
Time, continually splitting, continually repeats the original
break, the break from the beginning: the dividing of the eternal
present into a yesterday, a today, and a tomorrow, each different, unique. This continual change is the mark of imperfection,
the sign of the Fall. Finiteness, irreversibility, and otherness
are manifestations of imperfection. Each moment is unique and
distinct because it is separate, cut off from unity. History is a
synonym for Fall.

Contrasting with the heterogeneity of historic time is the
unity of the time which comes after all time. In eternity contradictions end, everything is reconciled, and in reconciliation
achieves perfection, its first and last unity. The coming of the
eternal present, after the Last Judgment, is the death of death—

the death of change. The affirmation of Christian eternity is
no less terrifying than the negation of India. In the third circle
of hell, where gluttons are suffering in a lake of excrement,
Dante meets a fellow countryman, a wretched man called
Ciacco. After prophesying new civic calamities in Florence—
reprobates have the gift of second sight—and asking Dante
to remind people of him when he returns to earth, poor Ciacco
sinks under the filthy water. "He will not come out again,"
says Virgil, "until the angelic trumpet sounds," which will be at
the last judgment. Dante asks his guide if after the "great
sentence" the affliction of this soul will be greater or milder.
And Virgil replies: He will suffer more because in a state of
greater perfection, both bliss and pain must be greater. At the
end of all time everything and every being will be more completely what they are: fullness of joy in paradise corresponds
exactly and point by point to fullness of suffering in hell.

The timeless past of the primitive, cyclical time, Buddhist
vacuity, dissolution of opposites in Brahman or in the Christian
eternity: the gamut of conceptions of time is immense, but
this variety may be reduced to a single principle. All these
archetypes, different though they may be, are attempts to
annul or, at least, minimize change. They confront the plurality
of real time with the unity of an ideal time, the otherness of
time with the identity of a time beyond time. The more radical
attempts such as Buddhist vacuity and Christian ontology
postulate conceptions in which the otherness and the contradiction inherent in the passage of time disappear altogether,
replaced by a timeless time. Other temporal archetypes tend
toward the harmonizing of contraries without suppressing

them completely, either by the conjunction of times in an immemorial past which continuously becomes the present, or by the idea of the cycles or ages of the world. Our era breaks abruptly with these ways of thought. Having inherited the unilinear and irreversible time of Christianity, it adopts the Christian opposition to cyclical conceptions but, simultaneously, denies the Christian archetype and affirms one that negates all the ideas and images of time which man has made for himself. The modern age is the first to exalt change and convert it into a foundation. Difference, separation, otherness, plurality, novelty, evolution, revolution, history—all these words can be condensed in one: future. Not past nor eternity, not time which is but time which is not yet and which always will be to come: this is our archetype.

At the end of the eighteenth century a Moslem Indian, Mirza Abū Tāleb Khan, visited England. On his return he wrote about his impressions. Among the things which surprised him most—together with the mechanical advances, the state of science, the art of conversation, and the English girls, ("earthly cypresses which suppress all desire to rest in the shade of the trees of Paradise")—one finds the idea of progress: "The English have very strange opinions as to what perfection means. They insist that it is an ideal quality based entirely on comparison; they say that humanity has risen gradually from the state of savagery to the exalted dignity of the philosopher Newton, but that, far from having reached perfection, it is possible that in future eras philosophers will regard the discoveries of Newton with the same disdain with which we now regard the rustic state of the arts among the savages." For Abū Tāleb our perfection

is ideal and relative. It does not have nor will it have reality; it
will always be insufficient and incomplete. Our perfection is
not that which is, but that which will be. The ancients feared
the future and invented formulas to exorcise it; we would
give our lives to know its shining face—a face we will never see.

2 The Revolt of the Future

In every society generations weave a web of repetitions and variations. In one way or another, explicitly or tacitly, the "quarrel of the Ancients and the Moderns" is renewed in each cycle. There are as many "modern periods" as there are historical epochs. Nevertheless, no society but ours has actually called itself "modern." If modernity is simply a consequence of the passage of time, to name oneself "modern" is to resign oneself to losing it very quickly. What will the modern era be called in the future? Perhaps to retard the inevitable erosion which obliterates everything, other societies decided to be known by the name of a god, a belief, or a destiny: Islam, Christianity, Middle Kingdom—these names refer to an immutable principle or, at least, to stable ideas and images. Every society settles on the name which is to become its foundation stone, defining itself in its choice and affirming itself with respect to others. Naming divides the world in two: Christians and Pagans, Muslims and Infidels, civilized men and barbarians, Toltecs and Chichimecans, ourselves and others. Our society also divides the world in two: the modern versus the old. This division works within society—where it creates the dichotomy between modern and traditional, new and old—and outside it.

Every time the Europeans and their North American descendants have encountered other cultures and civilizations, they have called them *backward*. This is not the first time a race or a civilization has imposed its forms on others, but it is certainly the first time one has set up as a universal ideal, not a changeless principle, but change itself. The Muslim or Christian based the alien's inferiority on a difference of faith; for the Greeks, Chinese, or Toltecs, he was inferior because he was a barbarian, a Chichimecan. Since the eighteenth century Africans or Asiatics have been inferior because they are not modern. The Western world has identified itself with change and time, and there is no modernity other than that of the West. There are hardly any barbarians, Infidels or Gentiles left; rather, the new Heathen Dogs can be counted in the millions, but they are called "underdeveloped peoples."

"Underdeveloped"—this adjective belongs to the anemic and castrated language of the United Nations. The word has no precise meaning in the fields of anthropology and history; it is not a scientific but a bureaucratic term. Despite its vagueness, or perhaps because of it, it is a favorite of economists and sociologists. Its ambiguity masks two pseudo-ideas: the first takes for granted that only one civilization exists, or that different civilizations may be reduced to a single model— modern Western civilization; the second affirms that changes of societies and cultures are linear and progressive and that they can be measured. The tendency to identify the modern age with civilization, and both with the West, has become so widespread that many people in Latin America talk about our cultural underdevelopment. How can a culture be underdeveloped? Is Shakespeare more "developed" than Dante, and is Cervantes "underdeveloped" compared with Hemingway? It is true that in the sphere of science there is an accumulation of knowledge, and in this sense one may speak of development. But this accumulation of knowledge in no way implies that today's men of science are more "developed" than yesterday's. It can be argued that at least when we speak of technology and its social consequences, the concept of development is justified. It is precisely in this sense that the concept seems to me equivocal and dangerous. The principles on which technology is based are universal; their application is not. The unthinking adoption of North American technology in Mexico has produced no end of misfortunes and a progressive degradation of our way of life and our culture. This is not nostalgic obscurantism; the only real obscurantists are those who cultivate the superstition of progress at any price. I know that we cannot escape; we are condemned to "development," but let us make the penalty less inhuman.

Development, progress, modernity—when did the modern era begin? Among the many ways we may read the great books of the past, there is one which I prefer: to look in them not for what we are, but for the thing which denies what we are. I return to Dante, precisely because he is the least up-to-date of the great poets of our tradition. Dante and Virgil pass through a huge expanse of flaming tombstones; it is the sixth circle of Hell where the Epicurean and materialist philosophers are burning. In one grave they meet a Florentine patrician, Farinata degli Uberti, who is enduring the torment of fire with courage. Farinata foretells Dante's exile, and then, answering a question by Dante, says that even the gift of second sight will be taken from him "When the door of the future is closed." After the Last Judgment there will be nothing to predict because nothing will happen. The closing down of time, the end of the future. Whenever I read this passage I seem to hear a voice not only from another age but from another world. And in fact it is another world which pronounces these dreadful words. The theme of the death of God has become a commonplace, but the idea that one day the gates of the future will close—sometimes I laugh at this idea; other times it makes me tremble.

We conceive of time as a continuous flow, an unending movement toward the future; if the future is closed, time stops. This idea is unbearable, intolerable. It offends our moral sensibilities by mocking our faith in the perfectibility of the species, and it offends our reason by denying our belief in evolution and progress. In Dante's world perfection is synonymous with a state beyond change and immobility, the plenitude of being. Removed from the changing and finite time of history, everything is what it is for ever and ever. Such an eternal present seems to us unthinkable and impossible; the present is by definition the instantaneous, and the instantaneous is the purest, most intense form of time. If the intensity of the moment becomes fixed in duration, we face a logical impossibility which is also a nightmare. For Dante the fixed present of eternity is the height of perfection; for us it is damnation, since it places us in a state which, if not death, is not life either. A kingdom of men buried alive, not in tombs of stone but in walls of frozen seconds. This perfection is a denial of existence as we have thought, felt, and loved it—as a perpetual possibility of being, movement, advance toward the changeable land of the future. There in the future, where being is a prescience of being, is our paradise. The modern era begins at the moment man dares accomplish an act which would have made Dante and Farinata degli Uberti tremble and laugh at the same time: opening the gates of the future.

Modernity is an exclusively Western concept which does not appear in any other civilization. Other civilizations postulate temporal images and archetypes from which it is impossible to deduce our idea of time, even as a negation. The Buddhists' vacuity, the Hindus' undifferentiated being, the cyclical time of Greeks, Chinese, and Aztecs, and the archetypal past of primitive man have no relation to our idea of time. Medieval Christian society conceived of time as a finite process, consecutive and irreversible; when time is used up—or, as the poet says, when the door of the future is shut—an eternal present will reign. In the finite time of history, in the here and now, man gambles with his eternal life. Our modern idea of time could appear only within this conception of irreversible time; and it could appear only as a criticism of Christian eternity. True, in the Islamic culture the temporal archetype is analagous to that of Christianity; but there, for a reason which will appear shortly, criticism of eternity could not possibly come about. And the very essence of modernity is the criticism of eternity: modern time is critical time.

History is conflict and every society is torn by social, political, and religious contradictions. Societies live and die because of them. One function of the temporal archetype is to offer an ideal and timeless solution to these contradictions and thus preserve the society from change and death. Therefore, every idea of time is a metaphor invented not by a poet but by a race. But these great collective images of time are converted into concepts by theologians and philosophers. Passing through the sieve of reason and criticism, they become versions, more or less well-defined, of the principle of identity. Sometimes the elimination of oppositions is radical: Buddhist criticism gets rid of the terms "I" and "the world," affirming universal vacuity, an absolute about which nothing can be said because it is empty of everything, including, says a Mahayana Sutra, its own emptiness. In other cases, contrary elements are not removed but reconciled and harmonized, as in ancient China's philosophy of time. The possibility that the contradiction will explode, destroying the system, is both intellectual and real. If logical coherence collapses, society loses its foundations and falls. Hence the closed and self-sufficient nature of these archetypes, their claim to invulnerability, and their resistance to change. A society may change its archetype—move, perhaps, from polytheism to monotheism, or from cyclical time to the finite and irreversible time of Islam or Christianity—but the archetypes are neither changed nor transformed. The single exception to this universal rule is Western society.

The Christian dichotomy results from the dual legacy of Judaic monotheism and pagan philosophy. The Greek idea of Being—in any of its versions, from the Presocratics to the Epicureans, Stoics, and Neoplatonists—is incompatible with the Judaic idea of a personal God who created the universe. Christian philosophy was deeply aware of this contradiction. It was its central theme from the Church fathers onward, and

Scholasticism tried to resolve it with an ontology of extraordinary subtlety. The modern age resulted from the impossibility of solving it. The dispute between reason and revelation also tore the Arab world apart, but there the victory went to revelation: the death of philosophy and not, as in the West, the death of God. Eternity's triumph shut the gates of the future, and identity won an absolute victory: Allah is Allah. The Western world escaped tautology only to fall into contradiction.

The modern age began when the conflict between God and Being, reason and revelation was considered insoluble. Contrary to what happened in Islam, reason grew at the expense of divinity. God is one and indivisible (He does not tolerate otherness except as the sin of non-being); meanwhile reason tends to split off from itself. Every time it reflects on itself, it divides in half; every time it contemplates itself, it discovers it is *other*. Reason aspires to unity but, unlike divinity, neither comes to rest nor identifies itself with unity; thus, the Trinity, which combines unity and plurality, is a mystery reason cannot penetrate. If unity becomes reflective, it becomes other: it perceives itself as otherness. By siding with reason, the West condemned itself to be always other, and to perpetuate itself only by constant self-negation.

In the metaphysical systems devised by the modern age in its early days, reason appears as a sufficient principle: it is its own foundation and a foundation for the world. But these systems were replaced by others in which reason is first and foremost criticism. Reason turned in upon itself ceased to create systems. It traced its limits, judged itself, and, by so judging, destroyed itself as a guiding principle. In this self-destruction reason found a new cornerstone. Critical reason, our ruling principle, rules in a peculiar way: rather than building systems invulnerable to criticism, it acts as self-critic. It governs insofar as it unfolds and sets itself up as the object of analysis, doubt, and negation. It is not a temple or a stronghold, but an open space, a public square and a road, a discussion, a method—a road continually making and unmaking itself, a method whose only principle is scrutiny of all principles. Critical reason, by its very rigor, accentuates temporality. Nothing is permanent; reason becomes identified with change and otherness. We are ruled not by identity, with its enormous and monotonous tautologies, but by otherness and contradiction, the dizzying manifestations of criticism. In the past the goal of criticism was truth; in the modern age truth is criticism. Not an eternal truth, but the truth of change.

The contradiction of Christian society was the opposition of reason and revelation, the Being which is thought thinking itself, and the God who is a creating persona. That of the modern age appears in the attempts to build systems based not on an atemporal principle but on the principle of change. Hegel called his philosophy a cure for division. But if the modern era is the schism of Christian society and if our very foundation, critical reason, continually divides itself, how can we be cured of division without denying ourselves and our foundation? The problem of the West was how to bring opposing elements into some kind of unity without eliminating them. In other civilizations, resolving the contradictions of opposites was the first step toward a unifying affirmation. In the Catholic world the ontology of the degrees of being also offered the possibility of attenuating oppositions to the point of making them disappear almost completely. Dialectic undertakes the same enterprise in the modern age, but does so through recourse to paradox—making negation the unifying bridge between terms. It claims to end antagonisms, not by reducing but by aggravating oppositions. Kant had called dialectic "the logic of illusions," but Hegel insisted that it was possible to eliminate the philosophical scandal known as the Kantian "thing in itself," thanks to the negativity of the concept. One need not agree with Kant to notice that, even if Hegel was right, dialectic abolishes contradictions only to have them reappear immediately. The last great philosophical system of the West oscillates between speculative delirium and critical reason; it is a thought which sets itself up as a system only to split in two, curing schism by schism. At one extreme of the modern age are Hegel and his materialistic followers, at the other, the criticism of all systems, from empiricism to Nietszche and modern linguistic and analytical philosophy. This opposition is the *raison d'être* of the Western world—its origin and its future death.

The modern age is a separation. I use "separation" in its most obvious sense: to move away from something, to cut oneself off. The modern age begins as a breaking away from Christian society. Faithful to its origins, it is a continual breaking away, a ceaseless splitting apart; each generation repeats the act by which we were founded, and in this repetition we deny and renew ourselves. Separation unites us with the original movement of our society, and severance throws us back on ourselves. As if it were one of those tortures imagined by Dante (but which is for us a stroke of luck: our reward for living in history), we search for ourselves in otherness, find ourselves there, and as soon as we become one with this other whom we invent and who is only our reflection, we cut ourselves off from this phantom being, and run again in search of ourselves, chasing our own shadow. This unending movement forward, always forward—toward what we do not know—we call progress.

Our idea of time as continuous change not only breaks with the medieval Christian archetype, but is a new combination of its elements: the horizontal time, from the Fall of Adam to the Last Judgment, and the eternal present which follows. The first element, finite time, becomes the almost infinite time of natural evolution and of history, but retains two properties: it is unrepeatable and it is sequential. The modern age rejects cyclical time in the same trenchant way Augustine did: things happen only once, they are unrepeatable. The main character of this temporal drama is no longer the individual soul but the collective entity, the human species. The second element, perfection embodied in eternity, becomes an attribute of history. Thus, for the first time, a value is placed on change. Beings and things do not reach the true fullness of their reality and perfection in the other time of the other world but in the present time—a time which is a fleeting and not an eternal present. History is our path to perfection. By virtue of its own logic, the modern age stressed not the actual reality of every man but the ideal reality of society and the species. If the acts and works of men ceased to have religious significance, they took on a superindividual coloration; their significance was primarily historical and social. This subversion of Christian values was also a conversion. Human time no longer revolves

around the motionless sun of eternity; instead it postulates
a perfection inside, not outside, history. The species, not the
individual, is the subject of this new perfection; it can be
reached not by fusion with God but through participation in
earthly, historical action. Perfection, regarded by scholasticism
as an attribute of eternity, is introduced into time; consequently,
the contemplative life is rejected as the highest human ideal,
and the supreme value of temporal action is affirmed. Man's fate
is not union with God, but with history. Work replaces peni-
tence, progress grace, and politics religion.

The modern age considers itself revolutionary. In many ways
it is; the first and most obvious is semantic: the modern world
has changed the meaning of the word *revolution*. The original
meaning—the turning of the worlds and the stars—has another,
now the more usual, placed beside it: a violent breaking with the
old order and the establishment of a new, more just, or more
rational order. The turning of the stars was a visible manifestation of circular time; in its new meaning, *revolution* became
the most perfect expression of sequential, linear, and irreversible
time. One implied the eternal return of the past; the other the
destruction of the past and the building of a new society. But
the first meaning does not disappear completely; it undergoes
yet another conversion. In its modern meaning, revolution
expresses with maximum coherence the concept of history as
inescapable change and progress. If society stops evolving and
grows stagnant, a revolution breaks out. If revolutions are
necessary, history is invested with the necessity of cyclical time.
This is a mystery as insoluble as that of the Trinity, since
revolutions are expressions of irreversible time and therefore

manifestations of critical reason. The ambiguity of the meaning of revolution reveals the mythic traces of cyclical time and the geometric traces of criticism, the oldest antiquity and the newest novelty. It is fate and it is freedom.

The great revolutionary change was the revolt of the future. In Christian society the future was under sentence of death, for the triumph of the eternal present, following the Last Judgment, was the end of the future. The modern age inverts the terms. If man is history and only realizes himself in history, if history is time looking forward and the future is the chosen place for perfection, if perfection is relative in relation to the future and absolute in relation to the past—then the future becomes the center of the temporal triad. It is a magnet for the present, a touchstone for the past. It is eternal like the fixed present of Christianity. Although our future is a projection of history, it is beyond history, far from change and chance. Like the eternity of the Christians, it lies on the other side of time; our future is simultaneously the projection of sequential time and its negation. Modern man is pushed toward the future with the same violence as the Christian was pushed toward heaven or hell.

Christian eternity was the solution to all contradictions and anguish, the end of history and of time; our future, though the repository of perfection, is neither resting-place nor end; on the contrary, it is a continuous beginning, a permanent movement forward. Our future is a paradise/inferno: paradise because it is the land of desire, inferno because it is the home of dissatisfaction. From one point of view our perfection is always relative; from another it is unattainable and untouchable.

The future, the promised land of history, is an inaccessible realm. We may apply to our own temporal archetype the criticism which the modern world makes of Christian eternity and that which Christianity brought to bear against the circular time of antiquity. The overevaluation of change entails the overevaluation of the future: a time which is not.

Is modern literature modern? Its modernness is ambiguous: the conflict between poetry and the modern world starts with the pre-Romantics and continues until today. I shall try to describe this conflict, not through its whole evolution—I am not a literary historian—but by stressing the moments and works which show it most clearly. If this method seems arbitrary, I claim only that I am not being gratuitously arbitrary. My views are those of a Hispano-American poet; this is not a detached dissertation but an exploration of my origins, an indirect attempt at self-definition. My reflections belong to what Baudelaire called "partial criticism," the only kind he considered valid.

I tried to define the modern age as an age of criticism, born from a negation. This negation shows itself with impressive clarity in our image of time. Christianity postulated the abolition of the future by conceiving eternity as the place of perfection. Modernity begins as a criticism of Christian eternity. Its criticism recombined the elements embodied in the Christian idea of time; the values of heaven and hell were transferred to earth and grafted onto history. Eternity was abolished; the future was enthroned in its place. Modernity sees itself ruled by the principle of change: criticism. This criticism, called *historical change*, adopts two forms: evolution and revolution. Both have the same meaning: progress; both are history and can be dated.

Critical negation encompasses both art and literature: artistic values are seen as separate from religious values. Literature declares its independence: the poetic, the artistic, the beautiful come to be self-sufficient values. The independence of artistic values led to the concept of art as *object*, which in turn led to a double invention: art criticism and museums. In the literary sphere, too, modernity expressed itself in a cult of the "object": the poem, the novel, the play. This trend began in the Renaissance and gained strength in the seventeenth century, but only as we approach the modern age do poets fully realize the nature of this idea: the writing of a poem implies the construction of a separate, self-sufficient reality. In this way the critical spirit is embodied *within* the creative process. This is not surprising, apparently: modern literature, as befits a critical age, is a critical literature. But the modernness of modern poetry seems paradoxical when observed closely. In many of its most violent and characteristic works—think of the tradition which runs from the Romantics to the Surrealists—modern literature passionately rejects the modern age. In another of its most persistent tendencies, embracing the novel as well as lyric poetry—that which culminates in a Mallarmé or a Joyce—our literature is an equally passionate and all-encompassing criticism of itself. Criticism of the subject of literature: bourgeois society and its values; criticism of literature as an object: language and its meanings. In both these ways modern literature denies itself and, by so doing, affirms, confirms, its modernness.

If modern literature begins as criticism of modernity, the figure in whom this paradox becomes incarnate is Rousseau. In his work the age which is beginning—the age of progress, inventions, and the development of capitalist economy—discovers one of its foundations and at the same time finds itself bitterly attacked. In the novels of Jean Jacques Rousseau and his followers, the continuous oscillation between prose and poetry becomes more and more violent, to the advantage not of prose but of poetry. Within the novel, prose and poetry join battle and this battle is the essence of the novel. The triumph of prose converts the novel into a psychological, social, or anthropological document; the triumph of poetry transforms it into a poem. In both cases it ceases to be a novel. In order to exist the novel must be a marriage of prose and poetry, without being entirely one or the other. In this difficult union prose represents the modern element: criticism, analysis. From Cervantes onward, prose seems gradually to win out, but at the end of the eighteenth century, a sudden earthquake wipes out the geometry of reason, a mist clouds the verbal glass. A new force, sensibility, upsets the constructions of reason. Not a new force, but rather a very old one, it predates reason and history itself. Against the new and the modern, against history and its dates, Rousseau opposes sensibility. It was a return to our origins, to the beginning of beginnings: sensibility lies beyond history and dates.

The Romantics turned sensibility into passion. Sensibility is an agreement with the natural world, passion a transgression of the social order. Both are Nature, humanized Nature; both are of the body. Although the passions of the flesh occupy a

central place in eighteenth-century literature, it is only with the
pre-Romantics and Romantics that the body begins to speak.
It speaks a language made up of dreams, symbols, and metaphors, a strange pact of the sacred with the profane and of the
sublime with the obscene. This is the language of poetry, not
of reason. It is radically different from that of the writers of the
Enlightenment. In the Marquis de Sade's work, the freest and
most daring of this period, the body does not speak, although
this writer's only theme is the body and its peculiarities and
aberrations. Philosophy speaks through these twisted bodies.
Sade is not a passionate writer; his raptures are intellectual
and his real passion is for criticism. He is not excited by the
postures of the bodies, but by the rigor and brilliance of
their dialectic. The eroticism of the other libertine philosophers
of the eighteenth century is not as boundless as Sade's, but
it is no less cold and rational. It is philosophy, not passion. The
conflict continues into our time: D. H. Lawrence and Bertrand
Russell fought against Anglo-Saxon puritanism, but no doubt
Lawrence found Russell's attitude to the body cynical, and
the latter found Lawrence's irrational. The same contradiction
exists between the Surrealists and the supporters of sexual
freedom. For the Surrealists erotic freedom was synonymous
with imagination and passion, while for the others it is only
a rational solution to the problem of the physical relationship
of the sexes. Georges Bataille believed that transgression was
the condition, even the essence, of eroticism; the new sexual
morality believes that if prohibitions are removed or attenuated,
erotic transgression will disappear or be lessened. Blake put
it this way: "Both read the Bible day and night / But thou
read'st black where I read white."

Christianity persecuted the old gods and geniuses of earth, water, fire, and air. It converted those it could not destroy: some were cast into the abyss where they were given a place in the bureaucracy of hell; others went to heaven and took their place in the hierarchy of angels. Critical reason depopulated heaven and hell, but the spirits returned to earth, to air, to fire, and to water—they returned to the bodies of men and women. This return is called Romanticism. Sensibility and passion are the names of the plural spirit which lives in rocks, clouds, rivers, and bodies. The cult of sensibility and passion is polemical. A double theme runs through it: the exaltation of Nature is as much a moral and political criticism of civilization as the affirmation of a time before history. Passion and sensibility represent naturalness: the genuine versus the artificial, the truly original versus the falsely new. Passion and sensibility belong to the world of origins—to the time before and after history, always identical with itself. The debasement of this original, sensitive, passionate time into history, progress, and civilization began, says Rousseau, when man first marked off a piece of land, saying to himself, "This is mine," and found people silly enough to believe him. History starts with private property. Fracture of primordial time: beginning of history, beginning of the history of inequality.

The modern nostalgia for an original time and for mankind reconciled with Nature is an attitude radically different from pre-Christian conceptions. Although, like the pagan world, it postulates the existence of a golden age before history, this age does not fit into a cyclical vision of time. The return to the happy age will be the result not of the revolution of the stars, but of the revolution wrought by men. The past does not return: men voluntarily and deliberately invent it and put it inside history. The past of revolutions is one form which the future assumes. The pagans believed in an impersonal Fate; the moderns believe in freedom, which is the direct heir of Christianity. The mystery which perplexed Saint Augustine— how to reconcile human freedom and divine omnipotence— has worried men since the eighteenth century. How far does history determine us and to what point can man channel and change its course? To the paradox of necessity and freedom another may be added: the criticism of modern society adopts the form of an act of violence. Revolution is criticism translated into action. At the same time revolution is the renewal of the original pact among equals, the restoration of a time prior to history and inequality. This restoration implies a negation of history, although such a negation will take place by virtue of an eminently historical act: criticism converted into revolutionary action. The return to primordial time, before history and inequality, represents the triumph of criticism. Thus we can say, however surprising the proposition may appear, that only the modern era can bring about the return to primordial time because only the modern era can deny itself.

Modern poetry, since its birth at the end of the eighteenth century, has embodied such a criticism of criticism. For this reason it seeks its foundation on a principle both antedating and antagonistic to, modernity. This principle, impervious to change and temporal succession, is Rousseau's beginning of the beginning, but it is also William Blake's Adam, Jean Paul's vision, Novalis' analogy, Wordsworth's childhood, Coleridge's imagination. Modern poetry affirms itself as the voice of this principle, and sees itself as the original word of foundation. Poetry is the original language of society, before all religious revelations; at the same time, it is the language of history and change: revolution. The principle of poetry is social and therefore revolutionary: it is the return to the original pact, before inequality. It is individual and belongs to every man and to every woman; it is the reconquest of original innocence. It opposes both the modern age and Christianity, but it is also a confirmation both of the historical time of the modern world (revolution) and of the mythic time of Christianity (original innocence). The theme of the establishment of another society is a revolutionary theme, which places in the future the time of the beginning; the restoration of original innocence is a religious theme which places the past before the Fall in the present. The history of modern poetry is that of the oscillation between revolutionary temptation and religious temptation.

3 Children of the Mire

At least half of the history of modern poetry is the story of the fascination poets have felt toward systems fashioned by critical reason. "Fascinate" in this context means bewitch, mesmerize— and deceive. As in the case of the German Romantics, repulsion inevitably followed attraction. This group is usually considered Catholic and monarchic, and hostile to the French Revolution. Nevertheless, initially most of them felt enthusiasm and sympathy for the revolutionary movement. Indeed, their conversion to Catholicism and to monarchic absolutism was as much the consequence of the ambiguity of Romanticism— always torn between two extremes—as of the nature of the historical dilemma faced by this generation. The French Revolution had two aspects: as a revolutionary movement it offered European nations a universal vision of man and a new conception of society and of the State; as a national movement it strengthened French expansionism outside the country, and, within, the policy of centralization begun by Richelieu. The wars against the Consulate and the Empire were simultaneously wars of national liberation and wars in defense of monarchic absolutism. For example, the Spanish liberals who collaborated with the French were loyal to their political ideas but disloyal to their country, whereas other Spaniards had to resign themselves to combining the cause of Spanish independence with that of the wretched Ferdinand VII and the Church.

Apart from political circumstances, the attitude of the German Romantics was far from conservative. Hölderlin comes to mind (though, like Blake, he is not strictly Romantic, and for the same reasons: chronologically both slightly antedate Romanticism and extend past it, to reach us today). In the days of the First Coalition against the French Republic (June 1792), he wrote to his sister: "Pray that the revolutionaries defeat the Austrians, for otherwise the princes will abuse their power dreadfully. Believe me and pray for the French who are the defenders of the rights of man." A little later, in 1797, he wrote an ode to Bonaparte—to the liberator of Italy, not to the general who was to turn, he charged scornfully in another letter, into "a sort of dictator." The theme of Hölderlin's novel *Hyperion* is dual: love for Diotima is inseparable from the establishment of a community of free men. The point of union between love of Diotima and love of freedom is poetry. Hyperion's struggle for his country's freedom is also his struggle to found a free society, and the establishment of this idyllic community implies a return to Ancient Greece. Poetry and history, language and community, poetry as frontier between divine and human speech—these oppositions became the central themes of modern poetry.

The dream of a free and egalitarian community, inherited from Rousseau, reappears among the early German Romantics, again linked with love, but more violently and sharply. They saw love as transgression of social bonds, and exalted woman not as erotic object but as erotic subject too. Novalis spoke of poetic communism, envisioning a society in which both the consumption and production of poetry would be a collective act. In *Lucinda* (1799), Frederick Schlegel made an apology for free love. His novel may seem naive today, but Novalis wanted to give it the subtitle, Cynical or Diabolic Fantasies. This phrase anticipated one of the most powerful and persistent currents of modern literature: the taste for sacrilege and blasphemy, the strange and the grotesque, the marriage of the commonplace and the supernatural, in short, the love of irony, that great invention of the Romantics. It is precisely irony, in Schlegel's sense of the word—love for the contradiction which lives in each of us, and awareness of this contradiction—that nourishes and destroys German Romanticism. This was the first and most daring of the poetic revolutions, the first to explore the underground regions of the dream, unconscious thought, and eroticism. It was also the first to turn nostalgia for the past into an aesthetic and a political program.

The English Romantics provide a similar example. While students at Cambridge, Southey and Coleridge conceived the idea of Pantisocracy as a free, egalitarian, communistic society which was to combine the "innocence of the patriarchal epoch" with the "refinements of modern Europe." The revolutionary theme of libertarian communism and the religious theme of the restoration of original innocence were thus interwoven. Coleridge and Southey decided to leave for America to found their pantisocratic society on the new continent, but the former changed his mind when he found out that Southey wanted to take a servant with him! Many years later Southey was visited in his Lake District retreat by the young Shelley and his first wife, Harriet. The old ex-Republican poet found his young admirer, "exactly as I was in 1794"; yet, writing of this visit to his friend Elizabeth Hitchener (January 7, 1812), Shelley says "Southey is a man corrupted by the world, contaminated by custom."

Wordsworth first visited France in 1790. A year later, when he was twenty-one years old and just down from Cambridge, his enthusiasm for the Republic took him back to France, where he spent two years, first in Paris and then in Orléans. He was a Girondin sympathizer. This fact, together with his revulsion at the revolutionary terror, explains his dislike of the Jacobins, whom he called the "tribe of Moloch." As many twentieth-century writers would do with the struggles of the Russian Revolution, Wordsworth took the side of one of the factions trying to take control of the French Revolution: the losing side. In his autobiographical poem *The Prelude*—with that hyperbolic style filled with capital letters which makes this great poet also one of the most pompous of his century—he describes one of the happiest moments of his life. It was a day in a town on the coast where "all that I saw or felt/Was gentleness and peace," and he heard a traveler recently landed from France say: "Robespierre is dead." He feels no less antipathy for Bonaparte, and in the same poem tells how, when he learned that the Pope had crowned Napoleon Emperor, he felt it was "This last opprobrium, when we see a people / . . . take a lesson from the dog / Returning to his vomit."

Faced with the disasters of history and the "degradation of the era," Wordsworth returns to childhood and its moments of translucency. Time splits in half, so that, rather than looking at reality, we look through it. What Wordsworth sees, as perhaps no one before or after him has seen, is not a fantastic world, but reality as it is: the tree, the stone, the stream, each firm, resting on its own reality in a sort of immobility which does not negate movement. These blocks of living time, spaces flowing slowly before the mind's eye, are a vision of the *other* time, a time different from the time of history with its kings and nations under arms, its revolutionary councils and its bloodthirsty priests, its guillotines and gallows. The time of childhood is the time of imagination, that faculty called by Wordsworth the "soul of nature," to signify that it is a power beyond the human. Imagination does not reside in man; rather it is the spirit of the place and of the moment. It is not only the power that allows us to see both the visible and the hidden aspects of reality, but also the means whereby Nature looks at herself through the poet's eyes. Through imagination Nature speaks to us and to herself.

The vicissitudes of Wordsworth's political passion can be explained in terms of his private life. His years of enthusiasm for the Revolution can be said to be those of his love for Annette (Anne Marie Vallon), a French girl whom he abandoned as soon as he started to change his political opinions. The years of his growing hostility for revolutionary movements coincide with his decision to leave the world and live in the country with his wife and sister Dorothy. But this simplistic explanation diminishes us, not Wordsworth. There is another explanation,

an intellectual and historical one that has to do with Wordsworth's political affinity for the Girondins, his repugnance
toward the *esprit de système* of the Jacobins, the moral and
philosophical convictions which led him to carry his Protestant
disapproval of papist universalism to revolutionary universalism,
and his Englishman's reaction to Napoleon's attempted invasion.
This explanation combines the liberal's antipathy for revolutionary despotism with the patriot's antagonism toward the
hegemonic pretensions of a foreign power, and, with reserva-
tions, can be applied also to the German Romantics. To consider
the conflict between the early Romantics and the French
Revolution as an episode in the clash between authoritarianism
and freedom is not totally false, nor is it completely true.

No, there is another explanation. The phenomenon is seen
time and again in different historical circumstances, throughout
the nineteenth century and afterward, with more intensity,
down to the present. It is hardly necessary to cite the experiences of Mayakovsky, Pasternak, Mandelstam, and so many
other Russian poets, artists, and writers; the polemics of the
Surrealists with the Third International; the bitterness of César
Vallejo, torn between loyalty to poetry and loyalty to the
Communist Party; the quarrels about "socialist realism" and —
but why go on? Modern poetry has been and is a revolutionary
passion, but this passion has been an unhappy one. There has
been attraction and rejection; and it is not the philosophers but
the revolutionaries who have banished the poets from their
republic. The reason for rejection is the same as for attraction:
both revolution and poetry attempt to destroy the present,
the time of history which is that of inequality, and to restore

the *other* time. But poetry's time is not that of revolution, the dated time of critical reason, the future of the Utopias; it is the time before time, the time of *la vie antérieure* which reappears in the child's timeless glance.

Poetry's ambiguity toward critical reason and its historical incarnations, the revolutionary movements, is one side of the coin; the other side is its ambiguity toward Christianity. Again, attraction and rejection. Almost all the great Romantics, heirs of Rousseau and eighteenth-century deism, were religion-oriented, but what were the actual beliefs of Hölderlin, Blake, Coleridge, Hugo, Nerval? One might ask the same question of those who openly declared themselves irreligious. Shelley's atheism is a religious passion. In 1810, in a letter to Thomas Hogg he writes: "O! I burn with impatience for the moment of Christianity's dissolution; it has injured me . . . I will stab the wretch in secret." This is odd language for an atheist and fore-shadows the Nietzsche of later years. Rejection of religion and love for religion: each poet invents his own mythology, and each mythology is a mixture of different beliefs, rediscovered myths, and personal obsessions. Hölderlin's Christ is a sun god, and in that enigmatic poem called "The Only One," Jesus turns into the brother of Hercules and of that Dionysus who "yoked his chariot to a team of tigers and went down to the Indus." The Virgin of the poems of Novalis is the mother of Christ and the pre-Christian Night, his fiancée Sophie, and Death. Nerval's Aurelia is Isis, Pandora, and the actress Jenny Colon, his unhappy love. The religions and loves of the Romantics are heresies, syncretisms, apostasies, blasphemies, conversions. Romantic ambiguity has two modes, in the musical meaning of the word: irony, which introduces the negation of subjectivity into the realm of objectivity; and anguish, which drops a hint of nothingness into the fullness of being. Irony reveals the duality of what seemed whole, the split in what is identical, the other side of reason; it is the disruption of the principle of identity. Anguish shows that existence is empty, that life is death, that heaven is a desert; it is the fracturing of religion.

The death of God is a Romantic theme. It is not philosophical but religious: as far as reason is concerned, God either exists or does not exist. If He exists, He cannot die; if not, how can someone who has never existed die? But this reasoning is only valid from the point of view of monotheism and the rectilinear and irreversible time of the West. The ancients knew that the gods were mortal; they were manifestations of cyclical time and as such would come to life again and die again. Up and down the Mediterranean coastline sailors heard a voice at night saying "Pan is dead," and this voice announcing the god's death also announced his resurrection. The Nahuatl legend tells us that Quetzalcoatl abandons Tula; immolates himself; becomes the double planet, Morning and Evening Star; and will one day return to claim his heritage. But Christ came to earth only once, for each event in the sacred history of Christianity is unique and will not be repeated. If someone says "God is dead," he is announcing an unrepeatable fact: God is dead forever. Within the concept of time as a linear and irreversible progression, the death of God is unthinkable, for the death of God opens the gates of contingency and unreason. There is a double reply to this: irony, humor, intellectual paradox; and also the poetic paradox, the image. Both appear in all the Romantics. The predilection for the grotesque, the horrible, the strange, the sublime, and the bizarre; the aesthetic of contrasts; the pact between laughter and tears, prose and poetry, agnosticism and faith; the sudden changes of mood, the antics—everything that turns each Romantic poet into an Icarus, a Satan, and a clown is essentially anguish and irony. Although the source of each of these attitudes is religious, it is a strange and contradictory sort of religion since it consists of the awareness that religion is hollow. Romantic religiosity is irreligious, ironic; Romantic irreligion is religious, anguished.

The theme of the death of God, in this religious/irreligious sense, appears for the first time, I think, in Jean Paul Richter. In this great precursor are merged all the trends and currents which will unfold in nineteenth- and twentieth-century poetry- and novel-writing—oneirism, humor, anguish, the mingling of genres, fantastic literature allied with realism and realism joined to philosophical speculation. Jean Paul's *Dream* is a dream of the death of God; its complete title is *Speech of Christ, from the Universe, That There Is No God* (1796). In an earlier version of the work, significantly, it is not Christ but Shakespeare who announces the news. For the Romantics, Shakespeare was the poet by antonomasia, as Virgil had been for the Middle Ages. Thus, when Jean Paul lets the announcement come from the mouth of the English poet, he forecasts what all the Romantics will say later: poets are clairvoyants and prophets through whom the spirit speaks. The poet replaces the priest, and poetry becomes a revelation rivaling the Scriptures. The definitive version of Jean Paul's *Dream* underscores the deeply religious character of this essential text, and, at the same time, its completely blasphemous nature. It is not a philosopher or a poet, but Christ himself, the son of God, who affirms that God does not exist. And the place where this is made known is a church in a cemetery. The time may be midnight, but how can one know for sure, since the face of the clock has neither numbers nor hands, and on its empty surface a black hand tirelessly traces signs which disappear at once and which the dead try in vain to decipher. Descending into the midst of the clamoring shades, Christ says: "I have explored the worlds, flown up to the suns, and I have found no God. I have been to the extreme limits of the universe, I have looked into the abyss and shouted 'Father, where are you?' but I heard only the rain falling into the depths and the everlasting tempest which no order governs." Dead children crowd around Christ and ask, "Jesus, have we no Father?" He replies, "We are all orphans."

Two themes are intertwined in the *Dream*: the death of the Christian God, the universal Father and Creator of the world; and the absence of a divine or natural order regulating the movement of the universe. The second theme directly contradicts the ideas spread by the new philosophy among the cultivated spirits of the time. Enlightenment philosophers had attacked Christianity and its God made man, but the deists as well as the materialists postulated the existence of a universal order. With few exceptions the eighteenth century believed in a cosmos ruled by laws which did not differ essentially from those of reason. An intelligent necessity, divine or natural, moved the world. The universe was a rational mechanism.

Jean Paul's vision manifests the exact opposite: disorder, incoherence. The universe is not a mechanism but a vast formlessness agitated in a way which without exaggeration can be called passionate. That rain which is falling from the very beginning into the endless abyss, and that everlasting storm on a landscape in convulsion are the very image of contingency. In this lawless universe, this world cast adrift, this grotesque vision of the cosmos, "eternity lies heavy upon chaos and when it consumes it, eternity is itself consumed." We have before us the "fallen Nature" of the Christians, but the relation between God and the world is inverted. It is not the world fallen from God's hand that casts itself into nothingness, but God himself who falls into the pit of death. This is an enormous blasphemy, at once irony and anguish. Philosophy had conceived a world moved not by a creator but by an intelligent order; for Jean Paul contingency is a consequence of the death of God. The universe is chaos because it has no creator. Jean Paul's atheism is religious and clashes with the atheism of the philosophers, for he replaces the image of the world as a mechanism with that of a convulsive world, endlessly in death throes yet never dying. In the existential sphere universal contingency is called orphanhood. And the first orphan, the Great Orphan, is none other than Christ. *Dream* scandalizes the philosopher as well as the priest, the atheist as well as the believer.

Jean Paul's dream was dreamed, thought, and suffered by many poets, philosophers, and novelists of the nineteenth and twentieth centuries: Nietzsche, Dostoevski, Mallarmé, Joyce, Valéry. It was known in France thanks to Madame de Staël's book *On Germany* (1814). There is a poem by Nerval, composed of five sonnets and entitled "Christ on the Mount of Olives" (1844), which is an adaptation of the *Dream*. Jean Paul's text is convulsive, abrupt, and exaggerated. The French poet does away with the confessional, psychological element. His is the account, not of a dream, but of a myth; not the nightmare of a poet in a cemetery church, but Christ's monologue before his sleeping disciples. A magnificent line, "le dieu manque à l'autel où je suis la victime" (There is no God at the altar on which I am the victim), in the first sonnet broaches a theme not found in Jean Paul and which the following sonnets bring to a climax in the very last line of all. It is the theme of the eternal return, which will reappear with unparalleled intensity and lucidity in Nietzsche, again associated with the theme of the death of God. In Nerval's poem, Christ's sacrifice in this godless world converts him into a new god—except that he becomes a divinity who has little in common with the Christian God. Nerval's Christ is an Icarus, a Phaëthon, a beautiful, wounded Attis whom Cybele brings back to life. The earth becomes intoxicated with this precious blood, Olympus collapses into the abyss, and Caesar asks the oracle of Jupiter Ammon, "Who is this new god?" The oracle is silent, for the only one who can explain this mystery to the world is "Celui qui donna l'âme aux enfants du limon" (He who breathed a soul into the children of the mire). This mystery is insoluble, for He who breathes a soul into the Adam of mud is the Father, the Creator, that very God who is absent from the altar where Christ is the victim. A century and a half later Fernando Pessoa faces the same enigma and his answer is somewhat similar to Nerval's. There is no God but there are gods, and time is circular: "Dios es un hombre de otro Dios más grande; / También tuvo caída, Adán supremo; / También, aunque criador, él fué criatura" (God is a man to another, greater God, and this greatest Adam also fell; Though the creator, he was a creature).

The poetic consciousness of the West has accepted the death of God as though it were a myth; or rather, this death truly has been a myth, not merely an episode in the history of our society's religious ideas. The theme of universal orphanhood, as symbolized in Christ, the great orphan and elder brother of the orphan children who are all mankind, expresses a psychic experience recalling the path of negation of the mystics. It is that "dark night" in which we feel ourselves adrift, abandoned in a hostile or indifferent world, guilty without guilt, and innocent without innocence. However, there is an essential difference: it is a night without an end, Christianity without God. At the same time, the death of God awakens in the poetic imagination a sense of mythic storytelling, and a strange cosmogony is created in which each god is the creature, the Adam, of another god. It is the return to cyclical time, the transmutation of a Christian theme into a pagan myth. An incomplete paganism, a Christian paganism permeated with anguish for the fall into contingency.

These two experiences—Christianity without God, and Christian paganism—have been basic elements of Western poetry and literature since the Romantic era. In both we face a double transgression. The death of God converts the atheism of the philosophers into a religious experience and a myth; in turn this experience denies its very origin: the myth is empty, a play of reflections on the lonely consciousness of the poet, for there is no one on the altar, not even Christ the victim. Anguish and irony: faced with the future time of critical reason and revolution, poetry affirms the nonsequential time of sensibility and imagination, original time. In the face of Christian eternity, it affirms the death of God, the fall into contingency, and the plurality of gods and myths. But each of these negations turns against itself: the time of the imagination is not a mythic but a revolutionary time; the death of God is not a philosophic but a religious theme, a myth. Romantic poetry is revolutionary, not with but against the revolutions of the century; and its religion is a transgression of religion.

In the Middle Ages poetry was the handmaiden of religion; in the Romantic era it was the true religion, the fountainhead of the Holy Scriptures. Rousseau and Herder had shown that language answered man's emotional rather than spiritual needs; not hunger but love, fear, or wonder made us speak. Humanity's first credos were poems. Whether we are dealing with magic spells, litanies, myths, or prayers, the poetic imagination is there from the start. Without poetic imagination there would be no myths or Holy Scriptures; at the same time, and also from the beginning, religion confiscates the products of poetic imagination for her own ends. The charm of myths does not lie in their religious nature—these beliefs are not ours—but from the fact that in them poetic storytelling transfigures the world and reality. One of the cardinal functions of poetry is to show the other side, the wonders of everyday life: not poetic irreality but the prodigious reality of the world. Religion takes over these visions, transforms works of imagination into beliefs, and beliefs into systems. But even then the poet gives perceptible form to religious ideas, transmutes them into images, and animates them: cosmogonies and genealogies are poems, Holy Scriptures are written by poets. Indeed, the poet is the geographer and the historian of heaven and hell: Dante describes the geography and the inhabitants of the other world; Milton tells us the true story of the Fall.

The critique of religion undertaken by eighteenth-century philosophy shattered Christianity as the basis of society. The fragmentation of eternity into historical time made it possible for poetry to conceive of itself as the real foundation of society. Poetry was believed to be the true religion and knowledge. Bibles, Gospels, and Korans had been denounced by the philosophers as bundles of old wives' tales and fantasies. At the same time, even materialists recognized that these tales possessed a poetic truth. In their search for a foundation predating revealed or natural religion, poets found allies among the philosophers. Kant's influence was decisive in the second phase of Coleridge's thought. The German philosopher had shown that between the sense data and the understanding, the particular and the universal, the "productive imagination" acted as intermediary. Through it the subject transcends himself: imagination projects and presents the objects of the sense data to the understanding. Imagination is the condition of knowledge: without it there could be no link between perception and judgment. For Coleridge the imagination is not only the necessary condition for all knowledge, it is also the faculty which converts ideas into symbols and symbols into presences.

Imagination is "a form of Being": no longer just knowledge but wisdom. Coleridge believed there was no difference between poetic imagination and religious revelation, except that the latter is historic and changing, whereas poets (insofar as they are poets, and whatever their beliefs may be) are not "the slaves of any sectarian opinion." He also said that religion was the "poetry of mankind." Years before, Novalis had written that "Religion is practical poetry" and poetry was the "first religion of humanity." There are many such quotations, all with the same meaning: Romantic poets were the first to affirm the historical and spiritual priority of poetry over official religion and philosophy. For them the poetic word is the founding word. In this bold affirmation lies the root of the heterodoxy of modern poetry in the face of religions and ideologies alike.

In the figure of William Blake are concentrated all the contradictions of the first generation of Romantics; they explode in an affirmation transcending Romanticism. Was Blake really a Romantic? Nature worship, one of the traits of Romantic poetry, does not appear in his work. He considered the world of imagination eternal, the world of generation finite and temporal. The first was mental, the other was a "vegetable glass" distorting our vision. These ideas seem to link him with the Gnostics, but his love for the body and his exaltation of erotic desire and pleasure ("sooner murder an infant in its cradle than nurse unacted desires") set him in opposition to the Neoplatonic tradition. Was he a Christian? His is not the Christians' Christ, but a nude Titan bathed in the radiant sea of erotic energy, a demiurge for whom imagining and doing, desire and satisfaction are one and the same. His Christ reminds us of Satan; his huge body, like a gigantic cloud lit by lightning, is covered with the flaming letters of the proverbs of Hell.

In the early years of the French Revolution, Blake used to walk about the streets of London with the blood-red Phrygian cap on his head. His political enthusiasm eventually waned, but not the ardor of his imagination, at once libertarian and liberating:

"All Bibles or sacred codes have been the causes of the following Errors: 1. That Man has two real existing principles: Viz: a Body and a Soul. 2. That Energy, call'd Evil, is alone from the Body; and that Reason, call'd Good, is alone from the Soul. 3. That God will torment Man in Eternity for following his Energies.
"But the following Contraries to these are True: 1. Man has no Body distinct from his Soul; for that call'd Body is a portion of Soul discern'd by the five Senses, the chief inlets of Soul in this age. 2. Energy is the only life, and is from the Body; and Reason is the bound or outward circumference of Energy. 3. Energy is Eternal Delight."

The violence of Blake's anti-Christian affirmations prefigured that of Rimbaud and Nietzsche. He attacked the rationalistic deism of the philosophers just as violently: Voltaire and Rousseau were victims of his anger, and in his prophetic poems Newton and Locke appear as agents of Urizen, the demiurge of evil. Urizen is the lord of systematic reason, inventor of the morality which imprisons men in its syllogisms, divides them

one against the other, and each against himself. Urizen: reason
without body and without wings, the great jailer. Blake not
only denounced the superstition of philosophy and the idolatry
of reason, but, in the century of the first industrial revolution
and in the country which was the cradle of this revolution, he
prophesied the dangers of the cult of progress. The landscape of
England was starting to change, and hills and valleys were
becoming covered with the vegetation of industry: iron, coal,
dust, and waste. He is in all things our contemporary.

   In Blake's contradictions and eccentricities there is a larger
coherence not found in any of his critics. Eliot charged his
mythology with being undigested and syncretistic, a private
religion made up of fragments of myths and eccentric beliefs.
One could accuse most modern poets of the same thing, from
Hölderlin and Nerval to Yeats and Rilke; faced with the progressive disintegration of Christian mythology, poets—not excluding
the poet of *The Waste Land*—have had to invent more or less
personal mythologies made up of fragments of philosophies and
religions. In spite of this diversity of poetic systems—rather, in
its very center—a common belief can be discerned. This belief
is the true religion of modern poetry, from Romanticism to
Surrealism, and it appears in all poets, sometimes implicitly but
more often explicitly. I am talking about *analogy*. The belief
in correspondences between all beings and worlds predates
Christianity, crosses the Middle Ages, and, through Neopla-
tionism, illuminism, and occultism, reaches the nineteenth century. Since then, secretly or openly, it has never failed to nourish
Western poets, from Goethe to Balzac, from Baudelaire and
Mallarmé to Yeats and Pessoa.

Analogy outlived paganism and will probably outlive Christianity and contemporary scientism. It has had a dual function in the history of modern poetry: it was the principle before all principles, before the reason of philosophies and the revelation of religions; and this principle coincided with poetry itself. Poetry is one of the manifestations of analogy; rhymes and alliterations, metaphors and metonymies are modes of operation in analogical thought. A poem is a spiral sequence which turns ceaselessly without ever returning completely to its beginning. If analogy turns the universe into a poem, a text made up of oppositions which become resolved in correspondences, it also makes the poem a universe. Thus, we can *read* the universe, we can *live* the poem. In the first case poetry is knowledge; in the second, it is action. In both it borders on philosophy and religion, but only to contradict them. The poetic image shapes a reality which rivals the vision of the revolutionary and that of the religious. Poetry is the *other* coherence, made not of reasons but of rhythms. And there is a moment when the correspondence is broken; there is a dissonance which in the poem is called "irony," and in life "mortality." Modern poetry is awareness of this dissonance within analogy.

Poetic mythologies, including those of Christian poets, grow old and become dust as do religions and philosophies. But poetry remains, and thus we can continue to read the Vedas and Bibles, not as religious but as poetic texts. Here again is Blake: "The Poetic Genius is the True Man . . . all sects of Philosophy are adapted from the Poetic Genius . . . the Religions of all Nations are derived from each Nation's different reception of the Poetic Genius." Although religions belong to history and perish, in all of them a nonreligious seed survives: poetic imagination. Hume would have smiled at such a strange idea. Whom can we believe? Hume and his critique of religion or Blake and his exaltation of imagination? For all the founders—Wordsworth, Coleridge, Hölderlin, Jean Paul, Novalis—poetry is the world of nonsequential time, the time of the body and of desire. Beginning word: founding word. But also disintegrating word, the breaking away from analogy through irony or anguish, through the awareness of history which in them is the knowledge of death.

4   Analogy and Irony

A literary movement, Romanticism was also a new morality,
a new eroticism, and a new politics. It may not have been
a religion, but it was more than an aesthetic and a philosophy:
a way of thinking, feeling, falling in love, fighting, traveling—a
way of living and a way of dying. Frederick Schlegel, in one
of his programmatic writings, said that Romanticism not only
proposed the dissolution and mixture of literary genres and
ideas of beauty, it also sought the fusion of life and poetry by
means of the contradictory but convergent actions of imagination and irony. Even more, its aim was to socialize poetry.
Romantic thought unfolds in two directions which end in
fusion: the search for that anterior principle which makes
poetry the basis of language and thus of society; and the union
of this principle with life and history. If poetry was man's
first language—or if language is essentially a poetic operation
which consists of seeing the world as a fabric of symbols and
relationships between these symbols—then each society is built
upon a poem. If the revolution of the modern age is the movement of society back to its origins, to the primordial pact of
equal with equal, then this revolution becomes one with poetry.
Blake said: "all men are alike in the Poetic Genius." Romantic
poetry, too, claims to be action; a poem is not only a verbal

thing, but a profession of faith and an act. Even the doctrine of "art for art's sake," which seems to deny this attitude, confirms and prolongs it, for it was an ethic as well as an aesthetic, and quite often implied a religious or political stance.

Romanticism was born almost simultaneously in England and in Germany, and spread throughout Europe like a spiritual epidemic. The pre-eminence of German and English Romanticism comes not only from chronological precedence, but from a combination of critical insight and poetic originality. In both languages poetic creation is interwoven with critical reflections on the nature of poetry, made with an intensity, originality, and penetration unparalleled in other European literatures. The critical texts of the English and German Romantics were true revolutionary manifestos, and established a tradition which continues today. The joining of theory and practice, poetry and poetics, was one more manifestation of the Romantic aspiration to unite the extremes—art and life, timeless antiquity and contemporary history, imagination and irony. By means of the dialogue between prose and poetry they tried to revitalize poetry by immersing it in everyday speech—and to idealize prose by dissolving the logic of discourse in the logic of the image. As consequences of this interpenetration, we see throughout the nineteenth and twentieth centuries the emergence of the prose poem and the periodic renovation of poetic language by increasingly strong injections of popular speech. But in 1800, as again in 1920, what was new was not so much that poets were speculating in prose about poetry, but that this speculation overflowed the limits of the old poetics, proclaiming that the new poetry was also a new way of feeling and living.

The union of poetry and prose is a constant among English

and German Romantics, although it is not visible in all poets with the same intensity and in the same fashion. In some, such as Coleridge and Novalis, verse and prose, despite their inter-communication, are clearly independent. We have *Kubla Khan* and *The Ancient Mariner* on one side, the critical texts of *Biographia Literaria* on the other; or the *Hymns to the Night* as opposed to the philosophical prose of the *Fragments*. In other poets inspiration and reflection blend equally in prose and verse. Neither Hölderlin nor Wordsworth is a philosophical poet, fortunately for them, but in both thought tends to turn into perceptible image. In a poet like Blake, the poetic image is inseparable from speculative thinking, and the frontier between prose and poetry cannot be distinguished.

Whatever the differences—and they are profound—which separate these poets, they all conceive of poetry as a vital experience involving the totality of the human being. A poem is not only a verbal reality; it is also an act. The poet speaks, and as he speaks, he *makes*. This making is above all a making of himself: poetry is not only self-knowledge but self-creation. The reader repeats the poet's experience of self-creation, and poetry becomes incarnate in history. Behind this idea lives the old belief in the power of words: poetry thought and lived as a magical operation destined to transmute reality. The analogy between magic and poetry, a recurring theme throughout the nineteenth and twentieth centuries, originates with the German Romantics. The conception of poetry as magic implies an aesthetic of action. Art ceases to be exclusively representation and contemplation; it becomes also an intervention in reality. If art mirrors the world, then the mirror is magical; it changes the world.

Baroque and Neoclassical aesthetics insisted on a strict division between art and life. Although their ideas of beauty were very different, both emphasized the ideal nature of a work of art. When Romanticism affirmed the primacy of inspiration, passion, and sensibility, it erased the boundary between art and life. The poem was a vital experience, and life acquired the intensity of poetry. For Calderón life is illusion and deceit because it has the duration and consistency of dreams; for the Romantics what redeems life from the horror of its monotony is that it is a dream. The Romantics see the dream as "a second life," a way to recover the true life, the life of primordial time. Poetry is the reconquest of innocence. How can we fail to see the religious roots of this attitude and its intimate relation with the Protestant tradition? Romanticism originated in England and Germany not only because it was a break with the Greco-Roman aesthetic, but because of its spiritual link with Protestantism. The inward nature of religious experience stressed by Protestantism, as opposed to the ritualism of Rome, supplied the psychic and moral preconditions for the Romantic upheaval. Romanticism was above all a turning inward of the poetic vision. Protestantism made the individual consciousness of each believer the theater of the religious mystery; Romanticism disrupted the impersonal aesthetic of the Greco-Roman tradition, and allowed the poet's ego to become the primary reality.

To say that the spiritual roots of Romanticism lie in the Protestant tradition may seem overly bold, especially if we remember the conversions of various German Romantics to Catholicism. But the true meaning of these conversions is clear if one considers that Romanticism was a reaction against eighteenth-century rationalism. The Catholicism of the German Romantics was antirationalism, and it was no less ambiguous than their admiration for Calderón. Their reading of the Spanish dramatist was more a profession of faith than a true reading; August Schlegel saw in him the negation of Racine, but he did not realize that Calderón's plays contain a rational order no less rigorous than that of the French poet, rather more so. Racine's theme is aesthetic and psychological: human passions; Calderón's theme is theological: original sin and human freedom. The Romantic interpretation of Calderón confused Baroque poetry and Catholic neoscholasticism with anticlassicism and antirationalism.

The literary frontiers of Romanticism are the same as the religious frontiers of Protestantism. These frontiers were primarily linguistic. Romanticism was born and reached maturity in countries whose languages did not originate in Rome. The Latin tradition, central in Western culture up to that time, was finally broken. Other traditions appeared: popular and traditional poetry from Germany and England, Gothic art, Celtic and Germanic mythologies. The rejection of the image of Greece provided by the Latin tradition caused the discovery (or invention) of another Greece—the Greece of Herder and Hölderlin, that will become Nietzsche's and our own. Dante's guide in Hell is Virgil, Faust's, Mephistopheles. "The Classics!" says Blake, referring to Homer and Virgil, "It is the Classics, not Goths or Monks, that desolate Europe with wars." And he adds: "Grecian is Mathematic Form but Gothic is Living Form." As for Rome: "a warlike State never can produce Art." From the Romantics on, the Western world recognized itself as a tradition differing from that of Rome, and this tradition is not single but multiple.

Linguistic influence unfolds on deeper levels. Romantic poetry was not only a change of styles, but a change of beliefs, and this is what distinguishes it radically from the other movements of the past. Neither Baroque nor Neoclassical art rejected the Western system of beliefs. To find a parallel to the Romantic revolution we must go back to the Renaissance, above all, to Provençal poetry. This last comparison is particularly revealing, because in Provençal as in Romantic poetry there is an undeniable relation, still not completely understood, between the metrical revolution, the new sensibility, and the central position occupied by women in both movements. In Romanticism, the metrical revolution consisted of resurrecting the traditional poetic rhythms of Germany and England. There is a reciprocal relation between the resurrection of rhythms and forms and the reappearance of analogy. The Romantic vision of the universe and of man was inspired by analogy. And analogy fused with prosody: it was a vision more felt than thought, and more heard than felt. Analogy conceives of the world as rhythm: everything corresponds because everything fits together and rhymes. It is not only a cosmic syntax, it is also prosody. If the universe is a script, a text, or a web of signs, the rotation of these signs is governed by rhythm. Correspondence and analogy are but names for universal rhythm.

Although analogical vision inspires Dante as well as the Renaissance Neoplatonists, its reappearance in the Romantic era coincides with the rejection of Neoclassical archetypes and the discovery of national poetic traditions. In unveiling their traditional poetic rhythms, the English and German Romantics resuscitated the analogical vision of the world and of man. It is impossible to prove a cause-and-effect relation between accentual versification and analogical vision, it is impossible also not to see that there is a historical relation between them. The appearance of the first, in the Romantic period, is inseparable from the second. Analogical vision had been preserved as an *idea* by the occultist, hermetic, and libertine sects of the seventeenth and eighteenth centuries; when English and German poets translated this idea of "the world as rhythm," they translated it literally, turned it into verbal rhythm, into poems. The philosophers had thought of the world as rhythm; the poets heard the rhythm. It was not the language of the spheres—although they thought it was—but the language of men.

The evolution of verse forms in the Romance languages is also an indirect proof of the correspondence between accentual versification and analogical vision. The relation between the versification systems of the Romance and Germanic languages is one of inverse symmetry. In the former, the stress of the accents is secondary to the syllabic meter, while in the latter the syllabic count is secondary to the rhythmic distribution of accents. Accentual versification is more akin to song than to discourse; the danger of English and German verse lies not in intellectual dryness but in lyric confusion. The distinctive feature of Romance prosody is just the opposite. The tendency to regularity, dominant since the Renaissance and fortified by the influence of French Neoclassicism, was a constant feature in versification systems down to the Romantic period. Syllabic versification easily turns into abstract measurement and, as the example of eighteenth-century French poetry shows, into discourse and reasoning in verse. Prose consumes poetry—not the lively, colloquial prose which is one of the sources of poetry, but the prose of oratory and intellectual discourse. Eloquence rather than song. By the beginning of the nineteenth century, the Latin languages had lost their powers of enchantment and could no longer be vehicles for thought as antidiscursive and essentially rhythmic as analogy.

If the resurrection of analogy coincided in Germany and in England with the return to traditional poetic forms, in Latin countries it coincided with the revolt against regular syllabic versification. In French this revolt was more violent and total than in Italian or Spanish because syllabic versification dominated French poetry more than it did other Romance languages. It is significant that the two great precursors of the Romantic movement in France were prose writers, Rousseau and Chateaubriand; analogical vision unfolds more readily in French prose than in the abstract meters of poetry. It is no less significant that among the central works of real French Romanticism we find *Aurelia*, Nerval's novel, and a handful of narrations by Charles Nodier. Finally, among the great creations of French poetry of the last century we find the prose poem, a form which realizes the Romantic desire to mix prose and poetry. Such a form could have developed only in a language in which the absence of tonic accents limits the rhythmic resources of free verse.

As for verse: Hugo unmade and remade the Alexandrine; Baudelaire introduced reflection, doubt, irony—the mental

caesura which rather than breaking the regular meter tends to
produce psychic irregularity, exception; Rimbaud experimented
with popular poetry, song, free verse. The prosodic renovation
ended in two contradictory extremes: the broken lively rhythms
of Laforgue and Corbière and the musical score/constellation
of *Un coup de dés*. Laforgue and Corbière had a profound
influence on the poets of both Americas, Lugones, Pound, Eliot,
and López Velarde. With Mallarmé was born a form which
belongs neither to the nineteenth century nor to the first half
of the twentieth century, but to the present. This haphazard
enumeration has only one purpose: to show that the general
movement of French poetry during the last century can be seen
as a revolt against traditional syllabic versification. The revolt
coincided with the search for the principle that rules the universe
and the poem: analogy.

I have already referred to "real French Romanticism."
Actually there are two: one is the official Romanticism of the
textbooks and histories of literature—eloquent, sentimental,
and discursive—exemplified by Musset and Lamartine; the other,
which for me is the real one, is made up of a very small number
of works and authors: Nerval, Nodier, Hugo in his last period,
and the so-called "minor Romantics." In fact, the true French
heirs of German and English Romanticism are the poets who
come after the official Romantics, from Gautier and Baudelaire
to the Symbolists. These poets give us a different version of
Romanticism. Different, and yet the same, because the history
of modern poetry is a surprising confirmation of the principle
of analogy: each work is the negation, the resurrection, and the

transfiguration of the others. In this way French poetry of the
second half of the last century—to call it Symbolist would be to
mutilate it—is inseparable from German and English Romanticism: it is its prolongation, but also its metaphor. It is a translation in which Romanticism turns back upon itself, contemplates
and supersedes itself, questions and transcends itself. This is
the *other* European Romanticism.

In each of the great French poets of this period the fan of
analogical correspondences opens and closes; in the same way,
the history of French poetry, from *Les Chimères* to *Un coup de
dés*, can be seen as a vast analogy. Each poet is a stanza in
that poem of poems which is French poetry, and each poem is
a version, a metaphor of this plural text. If a poem is a system of
equivalences, as Roman Jakobson has said—rhymes and alliterations which are echoes, rhythms which play with reflections,
identity of metaphors and comparisons—then French poetry as
a whole becomes a system of systems of equivalences, an analogy
of analogies. In its turn, this analogical system is an analogy of
the original Romanticism of both Germans and Englishmen. To
understand the unity of European poetry without violating
its plurality we must conceive of it as an analogical system. Each
work is a unique reality and at the same time a translation of
the others—its metaphor.

The influence of the occultists, Gnostics, Cabalists, alchemists,
and other marginal figures was also deeply felt by the French
poets. At times they drank from the same fountain as the
German Romantics (Jakob Böhme, for instance, was known in
France through Louis Claude de Saint-Martin.) The occultist
tradition, on the other hand, had become associated with

certain trends of libertine and revolutionary thinking. The transition from the erotic mysticism of a Restif de la Bretonne to the conception of a society moved by the sun of passional attraction was accomplished by one man: Charles Fourier. The figure of Fourier is as central to the history of French poetry as it is to the history of the revolutionary movement. He is no less contemporary than Marx—and I suspect will become more so. Like Marx, Fourier believes that society is ruled by force, coercion, and lies; unlike Marx, he believes that what unites men is passional attraction: desire. To change society means to free it of those obstacles which inhibit the operation of the laws of passional attraction: "The first science I discovered was the theory of passionate attraction . . . I soon recognized that the laws of passionate attraction conformed completely to those governing the attraction of matter as explained by Newton and Leibnitz, and that there was a *unity in the system of movement for both the material and the spiritual worlds*. I suspected that this analogy could be extended from general to particular laws, that the attractions and properties of animals, vegetables, and minerals were perhaps coordinated on the same plan as those of mankind and the stars. . . . And so I discovered the analogy of four movements: material, organic, animal, and social. . . . As soon as I realized the theories of attraction and unity of these four movements, I began to read the handwriting of Nature."

Offical criticism had ignored or minimized Fourier's influence. Now, thanks above all to André Breton, who was the first to identify Fourier as one of the magnetic centers of our time, we know that there is a moment when revolutionary thought

and poetic thought converge: the idea of passional attraction.
Fourier: a secret author like Sade, though for different reasons.
When we speak of the "visionary" Balzac—the author of *Louis
Lambert, Séraphita, La peau de chagrin, Melmoth réconcilié*—
we think primarily of Swedenborg's influence, completely
forgetting Fourier. Even Flora Tristán, a great forerunner of
socialism and women's liberation, commited the same injustice:
"Fourier was a follower of Swedenborg; by revealing the doctrine of correspondences, the Swedish mystic proclaimed the
universality of science and suggested to Fourier his beautiful
system of analogies. Swedenborg conceived heaven and hell
as systems moved by attraction and repulsion; Fourier wished
to realize on earth Swedenborg's heavenly dream and he converted the angelic hosts into phalansteries." Stendhal said:
"perhaps within twenty years Fourier's genius will be recognized." April 1973 brought the second centenary of his birth,
and we still do not know his work well. A little while ago
Simone Debout published a manuscript which had been hidden
by prudish disciples, *Le nouveau monde amoureux*. In this
work Fourier shows himself as a sort of anti-Sade and anti-
Freud, although his knowledge of human passions was no less
profound than theirs. Against the current of his own age and
of our own, against a two-thousand-year-old tradition, Fourier
maintains that desire is not necessarily deadly, as Sade affirmed;
and that society is not repressive by nature, as Freud thought.
It is scandalous in the West to contend that pleasure is good,
and Fourier is really a scandalous author, whereas Sade and
Freud confirm in a certain way—negatively—the pessimistic
vision of Christianity.

Baudelaire made analogy the center of his poetics. A center in continuous oscillation, shaken by irony, awareness of death, the idea of sin—by Christianity, in short. Perhaps this ambivalence (perhaps his political skepticism also) caused him to attack Fourier so harshly. But this harshness is impassioned, it is the other side of admiration: "One day Fourier came to show us, with rather too much solemnity, the mysteries of analogy. I do not deny the value of some of his minute discoveries, though I think his mind was too preoccupied to be able to reach an exactness of detail such that he could understand truly and totally the system he had sketched. . . . Moreover, he could have given us an equally precious revelation if, instead of the contemplation of Nature, he had offered us readings of many excellent poets." Basically Baudelaire is reproaching Fourier for not having written a system of poetics, that is, for not being Baudelaire, for not having made a poetic out of analogy. For Fourier the system of the universe (analogy) is the key to the system of society; for Baudelaire the system of the universe is the model for poetic creation. Mention of Swedenborg was unavoidable: "Swedenborg, who had a greater soul, has shown us that heaven is a gigantic human being and that everything—form, color, movement, number, perfume—in the spiritual as in the material realm—is meaningful, reciprocal and correspondent." This admirable passage shows the creative nature of true criticism: it begins with an invective and ends with a vision of universal analogy. However, we must remember that Novalis had previously said, "He who touches the body of a woman touches the sky," and that Fourier wrote, "human passions are animated mathematics."

Two ideas appear in Baudelaire's conception. Although the first is very old, in him it is an obsession. It consists in seeing the universe as a language, a script. But it is a language in unending movement and change: each sentence breeds another sentence, each says something which is always different and yet says the same thing. In his essay on Wagner, Baudelaire returns to this idea: "it is not surprising that true music suggests analogous ideas in different minds; it would be surprising if sounds did not suggest colors, if colors could not call up the idea of melodies, and if sounds and colors could not translate ideas. Things have always expressed themselves by reciprocal analogies, since the day God uttered the world as an indivisible and complex totality." (Baudelaire does not write that "God created the world," but that he "uttered" it—he *said* it.) The world is not an ensemble of things but of signs; or, rather, what we call things are in fact words. A mountain is a word, a river is another, a landscape is a sentence. And all these sentences are in continual change: universal correspondence means perpetual metamorphosis. The text which is the world is not one but many: each page is the translation and the metamorphosis of another page which is the same in relation to another, and so on ad infinitum. The world is the metaphor of a metaphor. The world loses its reality and becomes a figure of speech. At the heart of analogy lies emptiness: the multiplicity of texts implies that there is no original text. Into this void the reality of the world and the meaning of language together rush headlong and disappear. But it is Mallarmé and not Baudelaire who will dare to gaze into this void and convert this contemplation into the substance of poetry.

Nor is the other idea which obsessed Baudelaire any less dizzying: if the universe is a cipher, a coded language, "what is the poet, in the widest sense, but a translator, a decipherer?" Each poem is a reading of reality; this reading is a translation; this translation is a writing, a new code for the reality which is being unravelled. The poem is the universe's double: a secret writing, a space covered with hieroglyphics. To write a poem is to decipher the universe only to create a new cipher. The play of analogy is infinite. The reader repeats the poet's act; to read the poem is to translate it and, inevitably, to convert it into another poem. The poetics of analogy consists ultimately in conceiving literary creation as a translation; this translation is multiple and confronts us with a paradox: plurality of authors. The true author of a poem is neither the poet nor the reader, but language. I don't mean that language eliminates the reality of the poet and the reader, but that it includes and engulfs them. Poet and reader are two existential moments—if one may express it like this—of language. If it is true that they use language to speak, it is also true that language speaks through them. The idea of the world as a moving text ends, as I said before, in the plurality of texts; the idea of the poet as translator or decipherer leads to the disappearance of the author. But it was the twentieth-century poets, not Baudelaire, who made a poetic method out of this paradox.

Analogy is the science of correspondences. It is, however, a science which exists only by virtue of differences. Precisely because this *is not* that, it is possible to extend a bridge between this and that. The bridge is the word *like*, or the word *is*: this is like that, this is that. The bridge does not do away with distance: it is an intermediary; neither does it eliminate differences: it establishes a relation between different terms. Analogy is the metaphor in which otherness dreams of itself as unity, and difference projects itself illusively as identity. By means of analogy the confused landscape of plurality becomes ordered and intelligible. Analogy is the operation by means of which, thanks to the play of similarities, we accept differences. Analogy does not eliminate differences: it redeems them, it makes their existence tolerable. Each poet and each reader is a solitary consciousness: analogy is the mirror in which they are reflected. And so, analogy does not imply the unity of the world, but its plurality, no man's sameness, but his perpetual splitting away from himself. Analogy says that everything is the metaphor of something else, but in the sphere of identity there are no metaphors. Differences are obliterated in unity, and otherness disappears. The word "like" fades away: being is identical with itself. The poetics of analogy could appear only in a society based on criticism and eaten away by it. To the modern world of rectilinear time and infinite divisions, to the time of change and history, analogy opposes not an impossible unity but the mediation of a metaphor. Analogy is poetry's way of confronting otherness.

The two extremes which tear apart the consciousness of the modern poet appear in Baudelaire with the same lucidity—with the same ferocity. Modern poetry, he tells us time and again, is bizarre beauty: unique, singular, irregular, new. It is not Classical regularity but Romantic originality: it is unrepeatable and not eternal—it is mortal. It belongs to rectilinear time: it is each day's novelty. Its other name is unhappiness, awareness or finiteness. The grotesque, the strange, the bizarre, the original, the singular, and the unique—all these names from Romantic and Symbolist aesthetics are only different ways of saying the same word: death. In a world where identity— Christian eternity— has disappeared, death becomes the great exception which absorbs all others and eliminates rules and laws. The cure for the universal exception is twofold: irony, the aesthetics of the grotesque, the bizarre and the unique; analogy, the aesthetics of correspondences. Irony and analogy are irreconcilable. The first is the child of linear, sequential, and unrepeatable time; the second is the manifestation of cyclical time: the future is in the past and both are in the present. Analogy turns irony into one more variant of the fan of similarities, but irony splits the fan in two. Irony is the wound through which analogy bleeds to death; it is the exception, the fatal accident (in the double meaning of the term: necessary and deadly). Irony shows that if the universe is a script, each translation of this script is different, and that the concert of correspondences is the gibberish of Babel. The poetic word ends in a howl or in silence: irony is not a word, nor a speech, but the reverse of the word, noncommunication. The universe, says irony, is not a script; if it were, its signs would be incomprehensible for man, because in it the word death does not appear, and man is mortal.

In an oft-quoted sonnet, "Correspondences," Baudelaire said,

Nature is a temple of living pillars
where often words emerge, confused and dim;
and man goes through this forest, with familiar
eyes of symbols always watching him.

The words these tree-columns say are *confused*: man passes
through these verbal and semantic forests without fully understanding the language of things. We have lost the secret of
the cosmic language which is the key to analogy. Fourier
innocently said he read in the "magic book" of Nature, but
Baudelaire confesses that he understands the writing of this
book only confusedly. The metaphor which consists in seeing
the universe as a book is very ancient and appears also in the
last canto of Dante's *Paradise*. The poet gazes upon the mystery
of the Trinity, that is, the paradox of otherness, which is unity
and is still otherness:

In that abyss I saw how love held bound
Into one volume all the leaves whose flight
Is scattered through the universe around;

How substance, accident and mode unite
Fused, so to speak, together, in such wise
That this I tell of is one simple light.

The pluralities of the world—leaves blown here and there—come
to rest together in the sacred book; substance and accident
in the end are joined. Everything is a reflection of that unity,
not excluding the words of the poet who names it. In the next
tercet, the union of substance and accident is presented as a
knot, and this knot is the universal form enclosing all forms.
This knot is the hieroglyph of divine love. Fourier would
say that this love is none other than passional attraction. But
Fourier, like all of us, does not know *what* this center is, nor of
what it is made. His analogy, like Baudelaire's and that of the

moderns, is an operation, an "ars combinatoria"; Dante's analogy is based on an ontology. The heart of analogy is an empty space for us; this center for Dante is a knot, it is the Trinity which reconciles the One and the Many, substance and accident. Therefore, he knows—or thinks he knows—the secret of analogy, the key with which to read the book of the universe; this key is another book: the Holy Scriptures. The modern poet knows—or thinks he knows—precisely the contrary: the world is illegible, there is no book. Negation, criticism, irony, these also constitute knowledge, though of the opposite kind to Dante's. A knowledge which is not the contemplation of otherness from the vantage point of unity, but the vision of the breaking away from unity. An abysmal knowledge, an ironic knowledge.

Mallarmé closed this period and by so doing, opened our own. He closed it with the same metaphor of the book. In his youth, in the years of isolation in the provinces, he had the vision of the Work, a work he compared to that of the alchemists, whom he called "our forefathers." In 1866 he confided to his friend Cazalis: "I have confronted two abysms: one is Nothingness, which I reached without knowing Buddhism . . . the other is the Work." The work: poetry confronting nothingness. And he added: "perhaps the title of my volume of lyric poetry will be *The Glory of the Lie*, or *The Glorious Lie*." The title is revealing: Mallarmé wanted to resolve the opposition between analogy and irony. He accepted the reality of nothingness—the world of otherness and of irony is, after all, the manifestation of nothingness—but at the same time he accepted the reality of analogy, the reality of the poetic work. Poetry as the mask of nothingness. The universe resolves itself in a book: an impersonal poem which is not the work of the poet Mallarmé, vanished in the spiritual crisis of 1866, nor of anyone else. It is language which speaks through the poet, who is now only a transparency. Crystallization of language in an impersonal work which is not only the double of the universe, as the Romantics and Symbolists had wished, but also its abolition. The nothingness which is the world turns itself into a book: *the* Book. Mallarmé has left hundreds and hundreds of notes describing the physical characteristics of this loose-leaved book; the form in which its leaves will be distributed and combined at every reading so that each combination will produce a different version of the same text; the ritual of each reading with the number of participants and the price of entrance; the edition and sale of the book (odd calculations which remind us of Balzac and his financial speculations); he has left reflections, confidences, doubts, fragments, odds and ends—but the book does not exist; it was never written. Analogy ends in silence.

5   Translation and Metaphor

In France there was a Romantic literature—a style, an ideology,
some gestures—but there was no real Romantic spirit until the
second half of the nineteenth century, and this movement
was a rebellion against the French poetic tradition from the
Renaissance onward, against its aesthetic as much as against its
prosody; whereas English and German Romanticism was a
rediscovery (or invention) of their national poetic traditions.
What of Spain and her former colonies? Spanish Romanticism
was superficial and declamatory, patriotic and sentimental, an
imitation of French models, themselves bombastic and derived
from England and Germany. Not the ideas, just the topics; not
the style, just the manner; neither the vision of the correspondence between the macrocosm and the microcosm, nor the
consciousness that the "I" is a fault, a mistake in the system of
the universe. Not the irony, just sentimental subjectivity. There
were Romantic attitudes and there were poets not devoid of
talent and passion, who appropriated Byron's gesticulations
(not his economy of language) and Hugo's grandiloquence (not
his visionary genius). Not one among the official names of
Spanish Romanticism is of the first rank, with the exception,
perhaps, of Mariano José de Larra. But the Larra who fires our

imaginations is a critic of his times and himself, a moralist closer to the eighteenth century than to Romanticism, and the author of ferocious epigrams: "Here lies half of Spain; it died of the other half." The Argentinian Domingo Faustino Sarmiento, visiting Spain in 1846, told the Spanish: "You have no authors nowadays, nor writers, nor anything of any value . . . you over here and we over there *translate*." In Spain they were imitating the French, and in Spanish America they were imitating the Spanish.

José María Blanco White is the only Spanish writer of this period who deserves to be called Romantic. His family was of Irish origin, and one of his forefathers hispanized the surname simply by translating it: Blanco is White. I don't know whether Blanco White should be claimed for Spanish literature since most of his work was written in English. He was a minor poet and fittingly occupies a modest and chosen spot in some anthologies of English Romantic poetry. And yet, he was a great critic in the fields of history, morals, politics, and literature. His reflections on Spain and Spanish America are still valid. Blanco White represents a key moment in the intellectual and political history of the Hispanic nations. He has suffered as much from the hatred of conservatives and nationalists as from our neglect: a large part of his work has not even been translated into Spanish. Being intimately in touch with English thought, he was the only Spanish critic to look at our poetic tradition from the perspective of Romanticism: "Since Boscán and Garcilasco introduced Italian verse-forms in the middle of the sixteenth century, our best poets have been slavish imitators of Petrarch and the writers of that school . . . Rhyme, Italian meters, and a certain false idea of poetic language which only allows them to speak of what other poets have spoken of, have divested them of freedom of thought and expression." I have found no better or more concise description of the connection between the Renaissance aesthetic and regular syllabic versification. Blanco White not only criticizes eighteenth-century poetic models (French Classicism), but indicates their origin: the introduction of regular syllabic versification in the sixteenth century and, with it, an idea of beauty based on symmetry rather than personal vision. His remedy is the same as Wordsworth's: to renounce "poetic language" and use everyday language, to "think for ourselves in our own language." For the same reasons he laments continuing French influence: "It is an obvious misfortune that Spaniards, because of the difficulty of learning English, turn exclusively to French authors."

Two names seem to deny everything I have said: Gustavo Adolfo Bécquer and Rosalía Castro. The former is a poet admired by all; the latter is a writer no less intense than Bécquer and perhaps broader in scope and more energetic. (I hesitate to say more "virile"; energy is also womanly.) Both are late Romantics, late even for tardy Spanish Romanticism. Although contemporaries of Mallarmé, Verlaine, and Rimbaud, contemporaries of Whitman, their work shows them impervious to the movements that were shaking and changing their age. Nevertheless, they are true poets who close the prattling period of Spanish Romanticism and make us long for a Romanticism we never had. Juan Ramón Jiménez said that modern poetry in our language began with Bécquer. If this is so, it was too timid a beginning: the Andalusian poet reminds us too much of

Hoffmann and, conversely, of Heine. Neither Bécquer nor Rosalía Castro marks the end of one period or the dawn of another; they live in a twilight zone and do not on their own constitute an epoch.

Although Romanticism came late to Spain and Spanish America, the problem is not just chronological. This is not a new example of the "historical backwardness of Spain," that phrase used to explain the oddities of our nations, our eccentricity. Is the poverty of our Romanticism one more chapter on this theme for dissertations or elegies called "Spanish decadence"? It depends on our idea of the relation between art and history. Who can deny that poetry is a product of history? It is also oversimplification to consider it merely a reflection of history. The relation between them is more subtle and more complex. Blake said "Ages are all Equal but Genius is Always Above the Age." So extreme a point of view is not necessary; it is enough to recall that eras we regard as decadent are frequently rich in great poets: Góngora and Quevedo coincide with Philip III and Philip IV, Mallarmé lived in the Second Empire, Li Po and Tu Fu saw the collapse of the T'ang. So I shall try to outline a hypothesis which considers the reality of history as much as the reality of poetry, itself relatively autonomous.

Romanticism was a reaction against the Enlightenment, and was therefore determined by it; it was one of its contradictory products. An attempt of the poetic imagination to rekindle souls desolated by critical reason, a search for a principle different from religion and a negation of the sequential time of revolutions, Romanticism is the other face of modernity: its

remorse, its delirium, its nostalgia for a word made flesh.
Romantic ambiguity: it glorifies the powers and faculties of
the child, the madman, the woman, the nonrational *other*, but
glorifies them from the point of view of the modern era. The
primitive does not recognize himself as such nor does he want
to be primitive; Baudelaire goes into raptures at the "canni-
balism" of Delacroix precisely in the name of "modern beauty."
In Spain this reaction against the modern age could not appear,
because actually Spain did not have a modern age: she had
neither critical reason nor bourgeois revolution, neither Kant
nor Robespierre. This is one of the paradoxes of our history.
The discovery and conquest of America were no less determining
factors in the formation of the modern era than was the Reformation: if the latter provided the ethical and social bases for
capitalist development, the former opened the doors to European expansion and made possible the primitive accumulation
of capital in proportions unknown till that time. But the
nations which opened the era of expansion, Spain and Portugal,
remained on the fringe of capitalist development and did
not share in the Enlightenment. Since this exceeds the limits
of my subject I will not deal with it here; it is enough to recall
that from the seventeenth century on Spain became more and
more enclosed within herself and that this isolation gradually
resulted in petrification. Neither the action of a small elite
of intellectuals nurtured by eighteenth-century French culture
nor the revolutionary shocks of the nineteenth century succeeded in changing her. On the contrary, the Napoleonic
invasion strengthened monarchical absolutism and ultramontane Catholicism.

Spain's isolation was followed, brusquely and immediately, by a rapid decline of poetry, literature, and art. Why? Seventeenth-century Spain produced great dramatists, novelists, lyric poets, and theologians. It would be absurd to attribute the ensuing decadence to genetic mutation. Spaniards did not suddenly become stupid: each generation produces more or less the same number of intelligent people; what changes is the relation between the aptitudes of the new generation and the possibilities offered it by historical and social circumstances. During the seventeenth century Spaniards could not change the intellectual, moral, and artistic suppositions on which their society was based, nor could they take part in the general movement of European culture: in either case the danger to dissidents was a mortal one. Therefore, the second half of the seventeenth century was a time of recombining elements, forms, and ideas, a continuous returning to the same point to say the same thing. The aesthetic of surprise ends in what Calderón called the "rhetoric of silence." A resounding emptiness. The Spanish consumed themselves. As Sor Juana says, "They made a monument of their destruction."

With their reserves exhausted, Spaniards could choose no path other than imitation. The history of each literature and each art, of each culture, can be divided into fortunate and unfortunate imitations. The former are productive: they change the person who imitates and they change what is imitated; the latter are sterile. Spanish imitation was of the second kind. The eighteenth-century was a critical century but criticism was forbidden in Spain. The adoption of the French Neoclassical aesthetic was an act of external imitation which did not change the deep reality of Spain, or rather, left both psychic and social structures intact. Romanticism was the reaction of bourgeois consciousness to and against itself—against its own critical production: the Enlightenment. In Spain the middle class and the intellectuals voiced no criticism of traditional institutions or, if they did, it was insufficient. How could they criticize a modern era which they never had? Heaven, as the Spanish saw it, was not the desert which terrified Jean Paul and Nerval, but a place full of sugary virgins, chubby angels, beetle-browed apostles, and vengeful archangels—a fairground and an implacable court of law. Yes, Spanish Romantics rebelled against this heaven; but their rebellion, historically justifiable, was Romantic only in appearance. Spanish Romanticism, in an even more obvious way than French, lacks this element of originality, completely new in the history of Western sensibility—this dual element that we cannot avoid calling demoniacal: the vision of universal analogy and the ironic vision of man. Correspondence among all worlds and, at the center, the burnt-out sun of death.

Spanish American Romanticism was even more destitute than Spanish Romanticism: the reflection of a reflection. However, a historical circumstance affected our poetry, though not immediately, and made it change direction. I am referring to the Revolution of Independence. (I really should use the plural, for there were various revolutions, not all with the same meaning, but to avoid unnecessary complications I will deal with them as if they constituted a unified movement.) The Revolution of Independence in Spanish America was the revolution the Spanish never had, the revolution which failed time and again in the nineteenth and twentieth centuries. Ours was a movement inspired by the two great political archetypes of the modern era: the French Revolution and the American Revolution. One might even say that in this era there were three great revolutions with analogous ideologies: the French, the North American, and the Spanish American. Although all three succeeded, the results were very different: the first two created new societies, whereas ours initiated the desolation which has marked our history from the nineteenth century until today. Our principles were those of the Americans and the French, our armies defeated the Spanish absolutists, and as soon as Independence was achieved Republican governments were set up in our lands. And yet the movement failed: it did not change our societies and our liberators enslaved us.

Unlike the American Revolution, ours coincided with a state of extreme decadence in the seat of Empire. There are two attendant but not identical phenomena: the tendency of the Spanish Empire to fragment itself—a consequence of Hispanic decadence as much as Napoleonic invasion—and the movements toward autonomy of the Spanish American revolutionaries. Independence hastened the dismemberment of the Empire. The men who headed the liberation movements, with a few exceptions, lost no time in carving out nations to suit their own ends: the frontiers of each new country reached as far as did the army of the local chief. Later, oligarchies and militarism, in conjunction with foreign powers and especially North American imperialism, would complete the atomization of Spanish America. The new countries went on being the old colonies; social conditions remained unchanged, but now reality was hidden under layers of liberal and democratic rhetoric. Like false fronts, Republican institutions hid the old horrors and wretchedness.

The groups which challenged Spanish power used the revolutionary ideas of the time but were neither able nor willing to change our society: Spanish America was a Spain without Spain. As Sarmiento put it: the governments of Spanish America were the "executors of Philip II's will." Feudalism disguised as bourgeois liberalism, absolutism without a monarch but with petty kings—the presidents. And so the kingdom of the mask was born, the empire of lies. From then on the corruption of language, the semantic infection, became an endemic malady; lies became constitutional, consubstantial. Thence comes the significance of criticism in our countries. Philosophical and historical criticism for us is not only an intellectual function; it is like psychoanalysis. It is theory and praxis. If there is one urgent task in Spanish America it is the criticism of our historical and political myths.

Not all the consequences of the Revolution of Independence were negative. It freed us from Spain; and, if it did not change social reality, it changed our consciousness. It discredited forever monarchic absolutism and ultramontane Catholicism. The separation from Spain was an act of demythification: we were haunted by beings of flesh and blood, not the ghosts who kept the Spanish awake. Or were they the same ghosts with different names? In any case, the names changed and with them the ideology of the Spanish Americans. The rift with Spanish tradition widened in the first half of the nineteenth century, and in the second half became a clean break. The dividing knife was positivism. During these years the ruling classes and intellectual groups of Latin America discovered positivistic philosophy and embraced it enthusiastically. We changed the masks of Danton and Jefferson for those of Auguste Comte and Herbert Spencer. On the altars built by liberals to liberty and reason were placed science and progress, surrounded by their mythic creatures: the railroad and the telegraph. At that moment the paths of Spain and Spanish America diverged. The cult of positivism grew to become the official ideology, if not religion, of the governments of Brazil and Mexico; in Spain the best of the dissidents sought an answer to their anxieties in the doctrines of an obscure German idealist thinker, Karl Christian Friedrich Krause. No divorce could be more complete.

Positivism in Latin America was not the ideology of a liberal bourgeoisie interested in industrial and social progress, as it was in Europe, but of an oligarchy of big landowners. It was a mystification, a self-deceit as well as a deceit. At the same time it was a radical criticism of religion and of traditional ideology. Positivism did away with Christian mythology as with rationalist philosophy. The result might be called the dismantling of metaphysics and religion. This development was similar to the eighteenth-century Enlightenment; the intellectual classes of Latin America lived out a crisis to a certain extent analogous to that which had tormented Europeans a century earlier. Faith in science became tinged with nostalgia for the old religious certainties, and the belief in progress with vertigo at the prospect of nothingness. It was not complete modernity but its bitter foretaste: the vision of an uninhabited heaven, the dread of contingency.

Toward 1880 the literary movement called *Modernismo* appeared in Spanish America. Let me clarify my terms: Spanish American modernismo is, to a certain extent, the equivalent of French Parnassianism and Symbolism, and so has no connection with what in English is called "modernism." Modernism refers to the literary and artistic movements that began in the second decade of the twentieth century; as used by North American and English critics, it is what in France and the Hispanic countries we call *vanguardia*, the avant-garde. To avoid confusion I will use "modernismo" to refer to the Spanish American movement; in speaking of the artistic and poetic movements of the twentieth century I will use "avant-garde" and "vanguard," and for Anglo-American poetry, "modernism."

Modernismo was the answer to positivism, the criticism of sensibility—the heart and also the nerves—to empiricism and positivistic scientism. In this sense its historical function was similar to that of the Romantic reaction in the early days of the nineteenth century. Modernismo was our real Romanticism and, like French Symbolism, its version was not a repetition but a metaphor: the *other* Romanticism. The connection between positivism and modernismo is historical and psychological. We risk not understanding the nature of this relation if we forget that Latin American positivism, more than a scientific method, was an ideology and a belief. Its influence on the development of science was much less than its dominion over the minds and sensibilities of intellectual groups. Our critics and historians have been insensitive to the contradictory dialectic uniting positivism and modernismo. Consequently, they insist upon seeing the latter only as a literary trend and, above all, as a cosmopolitan and rather superficial style. No, modernismo answered spiritual needs. Or, more precisely, it was the answer of imagination and sensibility to the positivist drought. Only because it answered needs of the soul could it be a true poetic movement—the only one, in fact, among all those in our language during the nineteenth century, worthy of the name. The charge of superficiality can be more justly leveled at those critics who could not read within the lightness and cosmopolitan spirit of the *modernista* poets the signs (the stigmata) of spiritual exile.

For the same reason critics have been unable to explain fully why the modernista movement, which began as a voluntary adaptation of French poetry to our language, should have originated in Spanish America rather than in Spain. Certainly Spanish Americans have been and are more sensitive to what is happening in the world than the Spanish, less imprisoned within tradition and history. But this explanation is weak. Lack of information on the part of the Spanish? Rather, lack of *need*. From Independence onward, and especially from the adoption of positivism, the intellectual beliefs of the Spanish Americans differed from those of the Spaniards. Different traditions demanded different responses. Among us modernismo was the response needed to contradict the spiritual vacuum created by the positivistic criticism of religion and metaphysics; nothing was more natural than that Spanish American poets should be attracted by the French poetry of this period. They discovered in it not only the novelty of a language but a sensibility and an aesthetic impregnated with the analogical vision of the Romantic and occultist traditions. In Spain, on the contrary, the rationalistic deism of Krause was not so much a criticism as a substitute for religion—a timid philosophical religion for the use of dissident liberals—and therefore modernismo lacked the compensatory function it had in Spanish America. When modernismo finally reached Spain, some confused it with a mere literary import from France. From this mistaken interpretation, that of Unamuno, stems the idea of the superficiality of the modernista poets of Spanish America; others such as Juan Ramón Jiménez and Antonio Machado transposed it into the terms of the spiritual tradition in vogue among the dissident intellectual groups. In Spain modernismo was not a vision of the world but a language interiorized and transmuted by two great Spanish poets: Antonio Machado and Juan Ramón Jiménez (see Note 2). Again: a translation and a metaphor.

Between 1880 and 1890, almost without knowledge of each other, scattered throughout the continent—in Havana, Mexico City, Bogotá, Santiago de Chile, Buenos Aires, New York—a handful of young men began the great change. The center of this scattered fraternity was Rubén Darío, liaison officer, spokesman, and animator of the movement. In 1888 Darío coined the word modernismo to describe the new tendencies. Modernismo: myth of the modern age, or rather its mirage. What is it to be modern? It is to leave one's house, country, and language in search of something indefinable and unattainable, for it is confused with change. "He runs, he seeks. What does he seek?" Baudelaire wonders. And he replies: "He seeks something that we could call *modernity*." But Baudelaire does not define that elusive modernity and is content to call it the "singular element in every beautiful thing." Thanks to modernity, beauty is not one but many. Modernity distinguishes today's works from yesterday's, makes them different: "the beautiful is always strange." Modernity is that element which, by making it unique, gives life to beauty. But this life-giving process is a condemnation to capital punishment: modernity is the mark of death. The modernity which seduced the young poets at the close of the century is very different from that which seduced their fathers; it is not called progress nor are its outward manifestations the railroad and the telegraph; it is called luxury and its signs are useless and beautiful objects. Their modernity is an aesthetic in which desperation is linked with narcissism, and form with death.

The ambivalence of the Romantics and Symbolists in the face of the modern age reappears in the Spanish American modernistas. Their love of luxury and the useless object is a criticism of the world in which it is their lot to live, but this criticism is also a homage. Nonetheless, there is a radical difference between Europeans and Spanish Americans: when Baudelaire indicts progress as "a grotesque idea," or when Rimbaud denounces industry, their experiences of progress and industry are real, direct, whereas those of the Spanish Americans are derivative. The only experience of the modern age which a Spanish American could have in those days was of imperialism. The reality of our nations was not a modern one: not industry, democracy, or bourgeoisie, only feudal oligarchies and militarism. The modernistas depended on the very thing they abhorred; they swung between rebellion and abjection. Some, like Martí, were incorruptible and were sacrificed; others like

poor Darío, wrote odes and sonnets to tigers and alligators
in epaulets. But we who have seen and heard many great poets
sing the lofty deeds of Stalin in French, German, and Spanish
can forgive Darío for having written some stanzas in praise of
Zelaya and Estrada Cabrera, two Central American satraps.
An antimodern modernity, an ambiguous rebellion, modernismo was an act opposing tradition and, in its first stage, a
denial of a certain Spanish tradition. (I say a certain tradition
because at a second stage the modernistas discovered the other
Spanish tradition, the real one.) Their Gallic passion was a
form of cosmopolitanism; Paris was the center of an aesthetic,
rather than the capital of a nation. Their cosmopolitanism led
them to discover other literatures and to re-evaluate our Indian
past. The exaltation of the pre-Hispanic world, an aesthetic
first and foremost, was at the same time a criticism of the
modern age, especially of North American progress: Prince
Netzahualcoyotl confronting Edison. In this they were also
following Baudelaire, who had described the believer in progress
as "a poor wretch Americanized by zoocratic industrial philosophers." The recovery of the Indian world and, later on, of the
Spanish past, counterbalanced the admiration, fear, and anger
evoked by the United States and its policy of domination
in Latin America. Admiration for the originality and might
of North American culture vied with fear and anger at the
repeated intervention of the United States in the life of our
nations. I have referred to the phenomenon elsewhere; here I
will only emphasize that the anti-imperialism of the modernistas
was not exclusively based on political and economic grounds
but on the idea that Latin America and Anglo-Saxon America

represent two different and probably irreconcilable versions of Western civilization. The conflict was not only between classes and economic and social systems but between two visions of the world and of man.

Romanticism attempted a timid reformation of Spanish verse forms, but it was the modernistas who, by carrying it to extremes, finally succeeded. The metrical revolution of the modernistas was no less radical and decisive than that of Garcilaso and the Italianizers of the sixteenth century, although in the reverse direction. Contrary and unforeseeable consequences of foreign influences, Italian in the sixteenth century and French in the nineteenth century: in one case regular syllabic versification triumphed, while in the other continuous rhythmic experimentation provoked the reappearance of traditional meters and, above all, brought about the resurrection of accentual versification. At the beginning of the nineteenth century Andrés Bello, against the doctrine prevalent in Spain, had shown that Spanish verse depended not so much on syllabic regularity as on the play of tonic accents. (Here I must point out that it was Pedro Henríquez Ureña, the first Spanish American to hold the Charles Eliot Norton chair, who admirably compiled and systematized this doctrine.) Although the modernistas also devoted theoretic studies to the matter, it was their practice rather than their ideas that changed our verse. The modernista revolution resulted in the rediscovery of the original rhythms of our poetry. Its cosmopolitanism was in fact a return to the true Spanish tradition, denied or forgotten in Spain.

I have already indicated the connection between accentual

versification and the analogical vision of the world. The new rhythms of the modernistas brought about the reappearance of the original rhythmic principle of the language; this resurrection of meters coincided with the appearance of a new sensibility, which eventually proved to be a return to the *other* religion: analogy. Poetic rhythm is none other than a manifestation of the universal rhythm. Analogy is a rhythmic vision of the universe; before becoming an idea, it is a verbal experience. If the poet hears the universe as a language, he also *utters* the universe. As Baudelaire says, God uttered it. Return to cyclical time: the words of the poet, even when they do not expressly deny Christianity, dissolve it into vaster and more ancient beliefs. Christianity is no more than one of the combinations of universal rhythm. Christ's passion, as some poems by Darío say unequivocally, is no more than a momentary image in the rotation of ages and mythologies. Analogy comes to rest in syncretism. This non-Christian note was absolutely new in Hispanic poetry.

The influence of the occultist tradition among Spanish American modernistas was no less profound than among European Romantics and Symbolists. Our critics, although aware of this fact, seem to avoid it, as though it were shameful. Although scandalous, it is true: from Blake to Yeats and Pessoa, the history of modern poetry in the West is bound to the history of hermetic and occult doctrines, from Swedenborg to Madame Blavatsky. The influence of the Abbé Constant, alias Eliphas Levi, was decisive not only on Hugo but on Rimbaud. The remarkable affinities between Fourier and Levi, according to André Breton, are to be explained because both "place themselves in a vast current of thought which we can trace back to the Zohar and which disperses itself in the Illuminist schools of the eighteenth and nineteenth centuries. It is a trend of thought found in the idealist systems, in Goethe and, in general, in all who refuse to posit mathematical identity as the unifying ideal of the world" (*Arcane* 17). We know that the Spanish American modernistas—Darío, Lugones, Nervo, Tablada—were interested in occultist writings. Why has our criticism never pointed out the relation between Illuminism and the analogical vision, and between the latter and metrical reform? Rationalist scruples, or Christian scruples? In any case the relation is obvious. Modernismo began as a search for verbal rhythm and ended in a vision of the universe as rhythm.

Rubén Darío's beliefs vacillated, as we see in an oft-quoted line from one of his poems, "between the cathedral and the pagan ruins." I venture to modify it: between the ruins of the cathedral and paganism. Darío's beliefs, and those of most of the modernista poets are, more than beliefs, the search for a belief, and they evolve amid a landscape laid waste by critical reason and positivism. In this context paganism means not only Greco-Roman antiquity and its ruins but a living paganism: on one hand, the body, on the other, Nature. Analogy and the body are two extremes of the same belief in Nature. This affirmation opposes positivistic and scientific materialism as much as it does Christian spirituality. Ruins of the cathedral: the idea of sin, the awareness of death, the knowledge that man is fallen and exiled in this world and in the next, the vision of oneself as an accidental being in a world of contingency. Not a system of beliefs but a handful of fragments and obsessions.

The modernista tragicomedy is composed of a dialogue between the body and death, analogy and irony. If the psychological and metaphysical terms of this tragicomedy are translated into language, we find, not the opposition between regular syllabic versification and accentual versification, but the contradiction, more marked and more radical, between verse and prose. Analogy is continuously split open by irony, and verse by prose. The paradox beloved by Baudelaire reappears: behind the make-up of fashion, the grimace of the skull. Modern art knows itself to be mortal; there is its modernity. Modernismo becomes modern when it gains awareness of its mortality, that is to say, when it ceases to take itself seriously, when it injects prose into verse and makes poetry out of the criticism of poetry. This ironic, voluntarily antipoetic and therefore more intensely poetic note appeared precisely at the apogee of modernismo (Rubén Darío, *Cantos de vida y esperanza*, 1905) and is almost always linked with the image of death. But it was Leopoldo Lugones, not Darío, who initiated the second modernista revolution. With Lugones and his book *Lunario sentimental* (1909), Laforgue penetrated Hispanic poetry: Symbolism in its anti-Symbolist moment.

Our criticism calls the new tendency *postmodernismo*. This is not accurate. Postmodernismo was not what followed modernismo—which was actually vanguardismo—but a criticism of modernismo within the movement itself. It was an individual reaction on the part of various poets. Another movement did not start with them; modernismo ended with them. They were its critical consciousness, the consciousness of its ending. Moreover, the characteristic features of these poets—irony,

colloquial language—already had appeared in the leading
modernista poets. Finally, there is literally no space, in a chronological sense, for this pseudo-movement: if modernismo died
out around 1918 and the vanguardia began at about that time,
where can we put the *postmodernistas*? And yet the change
was remarkable. Not a change of values, but of attitudes.
Modernismo had populated the world with tritons and mer-
maids; the new poets traveled on commercial ships and landed
in Liverpool, not Cytherea; their poems were no longer songs to
old or new Romes but descriptions, rather bitter and reticent,
of middle-class districts; nature was not the jungle or the desert
but the village with its orchards, its priest and his "niece," its
girls "fresh and humble like humble cabbages." Irony and
prosiness: the conquest of the poetry of daily life. For Darío
poets are the "towers of God"; López Velarde sees himself
walking down an alleyway talking to himself; the poet as a
sublime, grotesque wretch, a sort of Charlie Chaplin "avant
la lettre." Aesthetics of the minimal, the near-to-hand, the
familiar. The great discovery: the secret power of colloquial
language. This discovery admirably served the purpose of
Lugones and López Velarde: to make the poem a psychological
equation, a meandering monologue in which reflection and
lyricism, song and irony, prose and verse are fused together and
separate, gaze at each other and are fused again. The song is
broken, the poem becomes an interrupted confession, the
melody is punctuated by silences and gaps. López Velarde put
it succinctly: "The poetic system has turned into a critical
system."

For reasons which I noted earlier, Spanish poets—except

Ramón del Valle Inclán, unique in this as in so many other things—could not make use of what constituted the true and secret originality of modernismo: the analogical vision inherited from the Romantics and the Symbolists. However, they immediately adopted the new language, rhythms, and metrical forms. Unamuno, for example, closed his eyes to these shining novelties which he judged frivolous. He closed his eyes but not his ears; meters rediscovered by modernistas reappear frequently in his verses. Unamuno's rejection is part of moderniso; it is not what went beyond Darío and Lugones but what confronted them. In his rejection Unamuno found the tone of his poetic voice, and in this voice Spain found the great Romantic poet she lacked in the nineteenth century. Although he should have been the predecessor of the modernistas, Unamuno was their contemporary and their complementary antagonist. Without the modernistas, Unamuno could not have been the poet we know. Poetic justice.

Spanish modernismo—I am thinking primarily of Valle Inclán, Antonio Machado, and Juan Ramón Jiménez—has more than one point of contact with Spanish American postmodernismo: criticism of stereotyped attitudes and precious clichés, repugnance toward falsely refined language, reticence toward antiquarian symbolism, search for a *pure* poetry (Jiménez) or an *essential* poetry (Machado). There is a surprising similarity between the voluntary colloquialism of Lugones, López Velarde, and some of the poems of Antonio Machado's first volume (*Soledades*, second edition, 1907). But soon the paths diverge; Spanish poets were less interested in exploring the poetic potential of colloquial speech—the music of conversation,

Eliot called it—than in renewing the melodies of traditional poetry. The two great Spanish poets of this period always confused spoken language with popular poetry. The latter is a Romantic fiction (Herder's "Song of the People") or a literary survival; the former is a reality, the living language of modern cities, with its barbarisms, its foreign words, its technical expressions, its neologisms. In its early stages Spanish modernismo coincided with postmodernista reaction against the literary language of Spanish America's first modernismo; later this opposition developed into a return to the Spanish poetic tradition: the song, the ballad, the copla. Thus, the Spanish confirm modernismo's Romantic nature, but at the same time they cut themselves off from the poetry of modern life. During these years Fernando Pessoa, through the voice of his heteronym, Alvaro de Campos, wrote:

Don't tell me there's no poetry in business, in offices!
Why, it seeps through every pore . . . I breathe it in the sea air
Because it's all got to do with ships and modern navigation,
Because invoices and commercial letters are the beginnings of
   history . . .
(Translated by Edwin Honig)

If the beginning contains the end, a poem by one of the initiators of modernismo, José Martí, sums up this movement and announces contemporary poetry. The poem is a premonition of his death in battle (in 1895), which it mentions as a necessary and, in a certain way, desired sacrifice.

Two Countries

I have two countries: Cuba and the night.
Or are they both one? As the sun's majesty
fades from the sky, I see her, Cuba,
dressed in veils, holding a carnation,
like a widow, quiet, sad.
How well I know that bleeding flower
trembling in her hand! My breast
is empty, it is destroyed and empty
where my heart was. It is time now
to begin to die. The night is good
for saying goodbye. Light
hinders, and human words. The universe
speaks better than man.
  Like a flag
that calls to battle, the red candle-flame
flares. Overflowing myself,
I open the windows. Mute, twisting
carnation petals, like a cloud
obscuring the sky, the widow Cuba passes . . .

(Translated by William Ferguson)

A poem without rhyme, written in hendecasyllables interrupted and broken by pauses for reflection, silences, human
breathing, and the breathing of the night. A monologue-poem
which escapes from song, an intermittent flow, a continuous
interpenetration of verse and prose. All the Romantic themes
appear in these few lines: the country and the night as two

women, death as the one and only woman, the one and only abyss. Death, eroticism, revolutionary passion, poetry: the night, the great mother, contains it all. Earth mother but also sex and common speech. The poet does not raise his voice, he speaks to himself when he speaks to the night and to revolution. Neither self-pity nor eloquence: "It is time now / to begin to die. The night is good / for saying goodbye." Irony is transfigured into acceptance of death. And, at the center of the poem, a phrase suspended between two lines, isolated in a pause to emphasize its weight—a phrase which no other poet in our language could have written before him (not Garcilaso, nor San Juan de la Cruz, nor Góngora, nor Quevedo, nor Lope de Vega)—because they were all possessed by the ghost of the Christian God and because they all faced the world as fallen Nature—a phrase which contains everything I have been trying to say: "The universe / speaks better than man."

6 The Closing of the Circle

The similarities between Romanticism and the twentieth-century avant-garde have been pointed out more than once. Both are movements of the young; both rebel against reason, its constructs and its values; both grant a cardinal place to the passions and visions of the body—eroticism, dream, inspiration; both attempt the destruction of visible reality in order to find or invent another one, magical, supernatural, and more than real. Two great historical developments alternately fascinate and tear them apart: for Romanticism, the French Revolution, the Jacobin Terror, and the Napoleonic Empire; for the avant-garde, the Russian Revolution, the purges, and Stalin's despotic bureaucracy. In Romanticism as in the avant-garde, the "I" defends itself from the world and finds its vengeance in irony or in humor, weapons which destroy the attacker as well as the attacked. The modern era denies and affirms itself in both movements. The artists as well as the critics were aware of these affinities. The Futurists, Dadaists, Ultraists, and Surrealists all knew that their rejection of Romanticism was itself a romantic act, in the tradition which Romanticism itself had inaugurated, that tradition which seeks continuity through rejection. But none of them realized the peculiar and truly unique relation of the avant-garde with earlier poetic movements. All were conscious of the paradoxical nature of their rejection, namely, that as they denied the past they prolonged it, and in so doing confirmed it; none of them noticed that, unlike Romanticism, whose rejection initiated this tradition, theirs brought one to a close. The avant-garde is the great breach, and with it the "tradition against itself" comes to an end.

Revolution/Eros/Meta-irony

The most remarkable similarity between Romanticism and the avant-garde, the crucial point of similarity, is the attempt to unite life and art. Like Romanticism, the avant-garde was not only an aesthetic and a language, but also an erotic and a political frame of reference, a world-view, an action: a life-style. The urge to change reality appears among the Romantics just as it does in the avant-garde, and in both cases it branches off in opposite yet inseparable directions—magic and politics, religious temptation and revolutionary temptation. Trotsky loved avant-garde art and poetry but he could not understand the attraction which André Breton felt for the occultist tradition. Breton's beliefs were no less strange and anti-rational than Esenin's. When the latter committed suicide, Trotsky wrote in a brilliant and impassioned article: "Our age is harsh, perhaps one of the harshest in the history of civilized humanity, so-called. The revolutionary is fiercely possessed by patriotic devotion to this era, his only true motherland. Esenin was no revolutionary . . .

he was a lyricist, gazing inward. Our era, on the other hand, is not lyrical. This is the fundamental reason why Sergio Esenin, of his own volition and so prematurely, has gone far from us and from this age" (*Pravda*, 19 January 1926). Four years later Mayakovsky, who was no "inward-gazing lyricist" and who was possessed by the revolutionary zeal of the era, also committed suicide, and Trotsky had to write another article—this time in the *Bulletin of the Russian Opposition* (May 1930). The contradiction between the era and its poetry, between the revolutionary and the poetic spirit, is vaster and deeper than Trotsky thought. Russia provides an exaggerated but not exceptional case. There the contradiction took atrocious shape: poets who were not murdered or who did not commit suicide were silenced by other means. The reasons for this hecatomb derive from Russian history—that barbarous past to which Lenin and Trotsky referred more than once—as much as from Stalin's paranoid cruelty. But equally responsible is the bolshevik spirit, heir to Jacobinism and its extravagant pretensions concerning society and human nature.

Poets reacted to the assault on Christianity by critical philosophy by becoming the channels through which the ancient religious spirit, Christian and pre-Christian, was transmitted. Analogy, alchemy, magic, personal syncretisms, and mythologies. At the same time, insofar as they were affected by the modern, poets reacted against religion (and themselves) with the weapon of irony. More than once—with irritation but not without true insight—Trotsky pointed out religious elements in the work of the majority of Russian poets and writers of the twenties—the so-called "fellow travelers." All of them, Trotsky says, accept the October Revolution as a *Russian* rather than a *revolutionary* fact. What is Russian is the traditional and religious world of the peasants and their old mythologies, "the witches and their spells," whereas the Revolution is the modern age: science, technology, urban culture. To support his criticism he quotes from Pilniak's *Naked Year*: "The witch Egorka says: 'Russia is wise in herself. The German is intelligent, but half-witted.' 'And what about Karl Marx?' asks one. 'He is German, I tell you, and therefore a half-wit.' 'And Lenin?' 'Lenin is a peasant, I mean a Bolshevik; therefore you have to be communists . . .' " Trotsky concludes that "it is very disturbing that Pilniak hides behind the witch Egorka and uses her stupid language, even on behalf of the communists." The early sympathy of these writers toward the Revolution—as is true for the Christian communism of Blok's *The Twelve*—"originates in a conception of the world which is the least revolutionary, the most Asiatic, most passive, and most heavily imbued with Christian resignation that can be imagined." What would Trotsky say if he read the Russian poets and novelists of today, equally possessed by that conception of the world, and now devoid of revolutionary illusions?

Nor did Trotsky regard as completely revolutionary a group which openly supported the Revolution, a branch of the pre-revolutionary Futurism which, headed by Mayakovsky, founded the LEF. "Futurism runs counter to mysticism, to the passive deification of Nature . . . And it favors technology, scientific organization, machines, social planning . . . There is a direct connection between this aesthetic 'rebelliousness' and social and moral sedition." But the Futurist rebellion had its roots in individualism: "The Futurists' exaggerated rejection of the past comes not from revolutionary proletarianism but from Bohemian nihilism." For this reason Mayakovsky's devotion to the Revolution, sincere though it may have been, seems to Trotsky a tragic mistake: "his subconscious feelings toward the city, Nature, the whole world, are not those of a worker but of a bohemian. *The bald lamppost that takes off the street's stockings*, a great image, reveals the poet's bohemian essence rather than anything else." Trotsky emphasizes "the cynical and shameless tone of many images" of Mayakovsky and, with admirable perspicacity, uncovers their Romantic origin. "Those thinkers who, in defining the social character of Futurism in its origins" (he is referring to the prerevolutionary period which was the most productive part of the movement), "place decisive importance on its violent protests against bourgeois life and art, reveal their own ingenuity and ignorance . . . The Romantics, both French and German, always spoke caustically about bourgeois morality and its hidebound life. They let their hair grow long, and Théophile Gautier wore a red waistcoat. The Futurists' yellow blouses are without doubt descendants of the Romantic waistcoat which aroused such horror among papas and mamas." How can we fail to recognise Romantic irony in the "cynicism and individualistic rebellion" of Mayakovsky and his friends? Russian literature of this epoch was torn between the "witches' spells" and the Futurists' satire. Avatars, metaphors of analogy and irony.

Trotsky's criticism amounts to a condemnation of poetry, not only in the name of the Russian Revolution but of the modern spirit in general. He speaks as a revolutionary who has adopted the intellectual tradition of the modern age "back from Marx to Hegel and to Adam Smith and David Ricardo." The roots of this tradition lie the French Revolution and the Enlightenment. And so his criticism of poetry, without his entirely being aware of it, takes on the form of the criticism which philosophy and science since the eighteenth century have made of the religion, myths, magic, and other beliefs of the past. Neither philosophers nor revolutionaries can patiently tolerate the ambivalence of poets who see in magic and revolution two parallel but not mutually exclusive methods of changing the world. The passages of Pilniak quoted by Trotsky echo what was said earlier by Novalis and Rimbaud: magic operates in a way not essentially different from that of revolution. The magic vocation of modern poetry from Blake to our own time is only the other side, the dark side, of its revolutionary vocation. Here lies the basis of the misunderstanding between revolutionaries and poets, which no one has been able to unravel. If the poet disowns his magic side, he disowns poetry and becomes a functionary and a propagandist. But magic devours its lovers, and a complete surrender to its powers can lead to suicide. The lure of death was called *revolution* by Mayakovsky; by Nerval, *magic*. The poet never escapes the double-edged facination; his concern, like that of Harry Martinson's tightrope-walker, is "to smile over the abyss."

The attack on poetry brings other condemnations to mind. With the same zeal that in the sixteenth and seventeenth centuries the church used to punish mystics, illuminati, and quietists, the revolutionary state has persecuted poets. If poetry is the secret religion of the modern age, politics is its

public religion. A bloodthirsty religion in disguise. The indictment of poetry has been a religious indictment: the revolution
has condemned poetry as heresy. Two-fold consequence of
the twilight of traditional religion: if in poetry a personal,
religious vision of the world and of man manifests itself, then
in revolutionary politics a double religious aspiration appears: to
change human nature, and to institute a universal church based
on a universal dogma. On the one hand analogy and irony; on
the other, the transposing of dogmatic theology and escatology
to the realm of history and society. The origins of the new
political religion—a religion unaware of itself—date back to the
eighteenth century. David Hume was first to notice it. He
showed that the philosophy of his contemporaries, especially
their criticism of Christianity, already contained the seeds of
another religion: to attribute an order to the universe and to
discover in this order a will and a finality meant incurring
religious illusion again. But although he predicted it, Hume did
not live to witness the descent of philosophy into politics
and its incarnation, in the religious meaning of the word, in
revolution. The epiphany of philosophic universalism adopted
the dogmatic and bloody form of Jacobinism and its cult of
the goddess Reason.

It is no coincidence that nineteenth- and twentieth-century
revolutionary movements have gone hand in hand with dogma-
tism and sectarianism; nor that, once in power, these movements
turn into inquisitions which periodically carry out ceremonies
reminiscent of Aztec sacrifices and *autos de fé*. Marxism began
as a "criticism of heaven," that is to say, of the ideologies
of the ruling classes, but victorious Leninism transformed this

criticism into a terrorist theology. The ideological heaven descended to earth in the guise of the Central Committee. The Christian drama between free will and divine predestination reappears in the debate between freedom and social determinism. Like Christian Providence, history reveals itself by signs: "objective conditions," the "historical situation," and other auguries and omens which the revolutionary must interpret. This interpretation, like that of the Christian, is at once free and determined by the social forces which substitute for Divine Providence. The exercise of this ambiguous freedom implies mortal risks: to be in error, to confuse the voice of God with that of the Devil, for the Christian means the loss of his soul, and for the revolutionary, historical condemnation. Nothing is more natural from this perspective than the deification of the leaders: the sanctification of texts as holy writings is inevitably followed by the sanctification of their interpreters and executors. In this way the age-old need to worship and be worshiped is satisfied. Suffering for the Revolution is the equivalent of the tortures joyfully accepted by the Christian martyrs. Baudelaire's maxim, slightly modified, suits the twentieth century perfectly: the revolutionaries have infused politics with the natural ferocity of religion (see Note 3).

The opposition between the poetic and the revolutionary spirit is part of a larger contradiction, that of the linear time of the modern age as opposed to the rhythmic time of the poem. History and the image: Joyce's work can be seen as a moment in the history of modern literature, and in this sense it is history; but the truth is that its author conceived it as an image—precisely as the image of the dissolution of the chronological time

of history in the rhythmic time of the poem. Abolition of
yesterday, today, and tomorrow in the conjoinings and couplings
of language. Modern literature is an impassioned rejection of
the modern age. This rejection is no less violent among the
poets of Anglo-American "modernism" than among the mem-
bers of the European and Latin American avant-gardes. Although
the former were reactionaries and the latter revolutionaries,
both were anti-capitalist. Their different attitudes originated in
a common aversion to the world of the bourgeoisie. Sometimes
the rejection was total, as in the case of Henri Michaux (distiller
of the poison/antidote against our time—against time). Like
their Romantic and Symbolist predecessors, twentieth-century
poets have set against the linear time of progress and of history
the instantaneous time of eroticism or the cyclical time of
analogy or the hollow time of the ironic consciousness. Image
and humor: rejections of the chronological time of critical
reason with its deification of the future. The rebellions and
misfortunes of the Romantic poets and their nineteenth-century
descendants are repeated in our time. We have lived alongside
the Russian Revolution, the bureaucratic dictatorships of
Communism, Hitler, and the *Pax Americana*, just as the Romantics were contemporary with the French Revolution, Napoleon,
the Holy Alliance, and the horrors of the first industrial revolution. The history of poetry in the twentieth century is, as it
was in the nineteenth, a history of subversions, conversions,
abjurations, heresies, aberrations. These words find their
counterparts in other words: persecution, exile, insane asylum,
suicide, prison, humiliation, solitude.

The duality of magic and politics is only one of the opposi-

tions with which modern poetry is laden. Love and humor
are another. All Marcel Duchamp's work revolves on the axis
of erotic affirmation and ironic negation. The result is *meta-
irony*, a sort of animated suspension, a region beyond affirmation and negation. The nude in the Philadelphia Museum, with
her legs open, clutching a gas lamp in one hand (like a fallen
Statue of Liberty), leaning back on bunches of twigs as if they
were the logs of a funeral pyre, against the background of a
waterfall (double image of mythic water and industrial electricity)—this is Artemis the pin-up seen through the chink of a
door by Acteon the voyeur. Meta-irony works in circular
fashion: the act of seeing a work of art is turned into an act of
voyeurism. Looking at something is not a neutral experience;
it is a confession of complicity. Our glance sets the object on
fire, and if we gaze, we ogle. Duchamp shows the creative
power of our look, and at the same time its derisory side. To
look is to transgress, but transgression is a creative game.
When we peep through a chink in the door of aesthetic and
moral censure, we glimpse the ambiguous relation between
artistic contemplation and eroticism, between seeing and
desiring. We see the image of our desire and its petrification in
an object—a naked doll. In the *Large Glass* Duchamp had presented the eternal feminine as a combustion engine and the
myth of the great goddess and her circle of victim-worshipers as
an electric circuit: the art of the Western world and its erotic-
religious images, from the Virgin Mary to Melusina, dealt
with in the impersonal manner of those industrial prospectuses
which show us how an apparatus works. The Philadelphia
assemblage reproduces the same themes, but from the opposite

perspective: not the transformation of Nature (girl, waterfall) into an industrial apparatus, but the transmutation of gas and water into an erotic image and a landscape. It is the reverse, the mirror image of *The Bride Stripped Bare by her Bachelors* — by her peeping-Toms. The other: the same.

Irony belittles the object; meta-irony is interested not in the value of objects but in how they work. And the way they work is symbolic: amor/umor/hamor . . . Meta-irony shows how mutually dependent are the things we call "superior" and "inferior," and forces us to withhold judgment. It is not an inversion of values but a moral and aesthetic liberation which brings opposites into communication. Duchamp closes the period which Romantic irony opened, and in this his work is analogous to that of James Joyce, that other poet of comic-erotic cosmogonies. Duchamp: critic of the subject who looks and of the object looked at; Joyce: critic of language and of that which speaks through language, man's myths and rituals. In both criticism becomes creation, as Mallarmé wanted; an act of creation which consists of the "renversement" of the modern era by means of its own weapons: criticism and irony. Industry, that most modern of all modernities, is also the most ancient, the other side of the myth of eroticism. It is the end of rectilinear time, or, more precisely, the presentation of linear time as one of time's manifestations. The two most extreme and "modern" works of the modern tradition also mark its limit, its end. With and in them the modern age, in its moment of fulfillment, closes.

Love/humor and magic/politics are variants of the central opposition: art/life. From Novalis to the Surrealists, modern poets have confronted this opposition and failed to resolve or dissolve it. Duality assumes other forms: antagonism between the absolute and the relative, or between the word and history. Disillusioned with history, Góngora changes poetry *because* he cannot change life; Rimbaud wants to change poetry *in order to* change life. It is almost always forgotten that *Soledades*, the poem which marks the consummation of Góngora's aesthetic revolution, contains a diatribe against commerce, industry, and especially the discovery and conquest of America, Spain's great historical feat. On the contrary, Rimbaud's poetry tends to spill over into action. The *alchemy of the word* is a poetic method of changing human nature; the poetic word antedates the historical event because it produces or, as he says, "multiplies the future." Not only does poetry provoke new psychological states (as do religions and drugs) and liberate nations (as do revolutions), it also has as its mission the invention of a new eroticism and the transformation of passional relationships between men and women. Rimbaud proclaims the need to "reinvent love," an endeavor which reminds us of Fourier. Poetry is the bridge between utopian thought and reality, the moment when the idea becomes incarnate. Poetry is the true revolution that will end the discord between history and idea. But Rimbaud left a strange testament: *A Season in Hell*. Afterward: silence.

At the other extreme, but intent upon the same adventure and as yet one more example of the common endeavor, Mallarmé looks for that convergent moment of all moments in which a pure act—the poem—can unfold itself. That act, those "dice thrown in eternal circumstances" is a contradictory reality because, though an action, it is also a poem, a non-act. And the place where the act-poem unfolds is a non-place: eternal circumstances, that is to say, non-circumstances. Relative and absolute merge without disappearing. The moment of the poem is the dissolution of all moments; and yet, the eternal moment of the poem is *this* moment: a unique, unrepeatable, historic time. The poem is not a pure act, it is a contingency, a violation of the absolute. The reappearance of contingency is, in its turn, only one moment in the spinning of the dice, now blended with the rotation of the worlds. The absolute absorbs chance, the uniqueness of this moment is dissolved in an infinite "total count in formation." As a violation of the universe the poem is also the double of the universe; as the double of the universe, the poem is the exception.

The art/life opposition, in any of its manifestations, is unresolvable. The only solution is the heroic-burlesque remedy of Duchamp and Joyce. Such a solution is a non-solution: literature becomes the exaltation of language to the point of annihilation; painting is criticism of the painted object and of the eye which looks at it. Meta-irony frees objects from their burden of time and signs from their meanings; it sets opposites in circulation; it is a universal animation in which everything turns back into its contrary. Not nihilism but disorientation: the side facing us is the side away from us. The game of opposites dissolves, without resolving, the opposition between seeing and desiring, eroticism and contemplation, art and life. Basically, this is Mallarmé's reply: the moment of the poem is the intersection between absolute and relative, an instantaneous reply which undoes itself ceaselessly. The opposition is always reappearing, now as the negation of the absolute by contingency, now as the dissolution of contingency in an absolute which, in turn, fades away. By the very logic of meta-irony, the non-solution which is a solution, is not a solution.

The Pattern Reversed

The avant-garde breaks with the immediate tradition—Symbolism and Naturalism in literature, Impressionism in painting—and this breach is a continuation of the tradition begun by Romanticism. A tradition in which Symbolism, Naturalism, and Impressionism had also been moments of breaking and of continuing. But something distinguishes the avant-garde movements from the earlier ones: the violence of the attitudes and the programs, the radicalism of the works. The avant-garde is an exasperation and an exaggeration of the trends which preceded it. Violence and extremism soon bring the artist face to face with the limits of his art or talent: Picasso and Braque explore and exhaust the possibilities of Cubism in a few years; in another few years Pound is on his way back from "Imagism"; Chirico moves from "metaphysical painting" to the academic cliché with the same speed that García Lorca goes from traditional poetry to neo-baroque Gongorism, and from this to Surrealism. Though the avant-garde opens new paths, artists and poets move along them so rapidly that in next to no time they reach the end and bump into a wall. The only remedy is a new transgression: make a hole in the wall, jump over the abyss. Each transgression is followed by a new obstacle, each obstacle by another jump. Always caught between extremes, the avant-garde intensifies the aesthetic of change initiated by Romanticism. Acceleration and multiplication: aesthetic changes cease to coincide with the movement of the generations, and occur within the life of the individual artist. Picasso is a good example: the dizzying and contradictory succession of breaks and discoveries which is his work confirms rather than denies the general direction of the age. While it is not certain that the twentieth century is richer in poetry and art works than was the nineteenth, it has undeniably been more varied and haphazard. But the acceleration of change and the proliferation of schools and trends has brought about two unexpected consequences: one undermines the very tradition of the change and the break, the other the idea of the "work of art." I will deal with both later.

Intensity and breadth. The accelerated pace of change is accompanied by the widening of literary space. Starting with the second half of the nineteenth century several great literatures begin to appear outside the strictly European sphere. The North American first, then the Slavic, especially Russian, and now those of Latin America, the Spanish-speaking nations and Brazil. In the philosophical and warlike American Indian, Chateaubriand discovers the *other*; in Edgar Allan Poe, Baudelaire discovers his mirror image. Poe is the first literary myth of the Europeans, by which I mean that he is the first American writer converted into a myth. But it is not really an American myth. For Baudelaire, who invented it, Poe is a European poet gone astray in the democratic industrial barbarism of the United States. More than an invention, Poe is

Baudelaire's translation. While he translates his stories, he translates himself: Poe is Baudelaire and Yankee democracy is the modern world, a world in which "progress is measured not by the use of gas lamps in the streets but by the disappearance of traces of original sin." (This odd opinion denies in advance Max Weber's idea: Capitalism is not the product of the Protestant ethic but anti-Christianity, an attempt to wipe out the original stain.) Baudelaire's vision will be that of Mallarmé and his descendants: Poe is the myth of the brother lost not in a strange and hostile land but in modern history. For all these poets the United States is not a country; it is the modern age.

The second myth was Walt Whitman, a different mirage. The Poe cult was one of similarities; the passion for Whitman was a double discovery: he was the poet of another continent and his poetry was another continent. Whitman glorifies democracy, progress, and the future. Judging from appearances, his poetry belongs to a tradition contrary to that of modern poetry: then how could he become such a powerful influence in world poetry? Some of Victor Hugo's poems contain a nocturnal, visionary element which at times redeems it of its eloquence and its facile optimism. And Whitman's? He has been called the poet of space—poet of space in movement, one should add. Spaces which are nomadic, an imminent future: Utopia and Americanism. But also, and primordially, language, the physical reality of words, images, rhythms. Whitman's language is a body, an all-powerful manifold presence. Without it his poetry would remain oratory, sermonizing, newspaper editorial, proclamation. Poetry filled with ideas and pseudo-ideas, commonplaces and authentic revelations, an enormous frothy mass which suddenly is incarnate in a body language that we can see, smell, touch, and, above all, hear. The future disappears; the present, the presence of the body, remains. Whitman's influence has been vast and has worked in all directions and upon opposed temperaments, Claudel at one extreme and, at the other, García Lorca. His shadow covers the European continent from Pessoa's Lisbon to the Moscow of the Russian Futurists. Whitman is the grandfather of the European and Latin American avant-garde. He makes an early appearance among us: José Martí presented him to the Spanish American public in an article written in 1887. Rubén Darío was immediately tempted to emulate him—a fatal temptation. Since then he has continued to excite many of our poets: emulation, admiration, enthusiasm, empty clatter.

The first manifestations of the avant-garde were cosmopolitan and polyglot. Marinetti writes his manifestos in French and polemicizes with the Russian Cubo-Futurists in Moscow and St. Petersburg; Khlebnikov and his friends invent *zaum*, the transrational language; Duchamp exhibits in New York and plays chess in Buenos Aires; Picabia works—and shocks—in New York, Barcelona, and Paris; Arthur Cravan refuses to duel with Apollinaire in Paris, but boxes in Madrid with black champion Jack Johnson, enters Mexico during the Revolution, and sails off on a barge, disappearing, like Quetzalcoatl, in the Gulf of Mexico; Cendrars' early poems report on Christmas in New York and an interminable journey on the Trans-Siberian; Diego Rivera meets Ilya Ehrenburg in Montparnasse and reappears a few years later in the pages of *Julio Jurenito*; Vicente Huidobro arrives in Paris from Chile, collaborates with the poets who were then calling themselves Cubists, and with Pierre Reverdy founds *Nord-Sud*. The Dada explosion compounds the babel: Arp is French-Alsatian; Ball and Huelsenbeck, German; Tzara, Romanian; and Picabia, French-Cuban. Bilingualism prevails— Arp writes in German and in French, Ungaretti in Italian and French, Huidobro in Spanish and French. Their predilection for French reveals the central role played in the evolution of modern poetry by the French avant-garde. I mention this well-known fact because some North American and English critics tend to ignore it. And even poets do. In a 1961 interview Pound made this extravagant affirmation: "If Paris had been as interesting as Italy in 1924, I would have stayed in Paris."

The avant-garde movement in English began a little later than on the continent and in Latin America. The first books of Pound and Eliot were impregnated with Laforgue, Corbière, and even Gautier. While the English language poets lingered in Imagism, a timid reaction to Symbolism, Apollinaire was publishing *Alcools*, and Max Jacob was transforming the prose poem. The great creative period of the Anglo-American avant-garde starts with the definitive version of the first *Cantos* (1924), *The Waste Land* (1922), and a little, magnetic, not very well known book by William Carlos Williams, *Kora in Hell: Improvisations* (1920). All this coincides with the beginning of the second stage of the European avant-garde: Surrealism. Two opposite versions of the modern movement, one red and the other white.

My purpose has been to show, first, the cosmopolitan nature of the avant-garde, and, second, that the poetry written in

English is part of a general trend. The dates indicate how un-
likely are affirmations that Eliot and Pound knew only the
Symbolist tradition and skimmed over Apollinaire, Reverdy,
Dada, and Surrealism. Harry Levin has pointed out to me the
influence of Apollinaire on e. e. cummings (who was, moreover,
the friend and translator of Aragon); the relation between *Kora
in Hell* and *Les champs magnétiques*, the prose-poem of André
Breton and Philippe Soupault is direct; Wallace Stevens had
an admirable acquaintance with contemporary French poetry—
but we would like to know more about those years when the
great change was coming about. The Paris of Pound and Eliot
was the cosmopolitan Paris of the first third of the century,
scene of many an artistic and literary revolution. The story of
Laforgue's influence on Eliot has been repeated to satiety; on
the other hand no one has explored the similarities between the
poetic *collage* of Pound and Eliot and the "simultanéiste"
structure of *Zone, Le musicien de Saint-Merry*, and other
Apollinaire poems. I am not trying to deny the originality of
the Anglo-American poets, but merely to indicate that the
movement of poetry in English can be fully understood only
within the context of Western poetry. The same applies to other
trends: without Dada, born in Zurich and translated into French
by Tzara, Surrealism would be inexplicable. Without Dada, and
without German Romanticism likewise. In their turn, the
Spanish and Argentinian ultraísmos cannot be explained without
Huidobro, who is inexplicable without Reverdy.

I have given these examples not to propose a linear idea of
literary history but rather to emphasize its complexity and its
transnational character. A literature is a language existing

not in isolation but in constant relation with other languages, other literatures. Eliot finds that the union of contradictory or disparate experiences is characteristic of the English "metaphysical" poets. A characteristic is not an exclusive trait: the union of opposites—paradox and metaphor—appears in all European poetry of that era. The consequent dissociation of sensibility and imagination—Neoclassic wit and romantic Miltonian eloquence—is also a general European phenomenon. For this reason Eliot can say that "Jules Laforgue, and Tristan Corbière in many of his poems, are nearer to the 'school of Donne' than any modern English poet." He might have said the same of López Velarde, had he been able to read him. Western literature is an interweaving of relationships, a fabric made up of the patterns traced by the weaving in and out of movements, personalities—and chance. Twentieth-century trends of poetry repeat patterns delineated by Romanticism but, as I shall try to show, in reverse. It is the same pattern—inverted. The relation of opposition between Germanic and Romance languages reappears in the twentieth century and tends to become crystallized at two extremes: poetry in English, and French poetry. I will refer to poetry in Spanish, not only because it is my own tradition but because the modern period, in Spain as in America, is one of the richest in our history. I realize that I am overlooking important movements and great figures: Italian and Russian Futurism, German Expressionism, Rilke, Benn, Pessoa, Montale, Ungaretti, the Greeks, the Brazilians, the Poles. . . The outlook of a German or Italian poet would undoubtedly be different. My point of view is a biased one, that of a Spanish American.

*

The term "modern poetry" is generally used in one of two
ways, one narrow, the other broad. It can refer only to the
period that began with symbolism and ended with the avant-
guard. Most critics take this period to have begun with Charles
Baudelaire. Some add a few more names, Edgar Allen Poe, for
example, or the Nerval of *Les Chimères*. Used more broadly,
as in this book, modern poetry is born at the end of the eighteenth century with the first Romantics and their immediate precursors, lives through the nineteenth and on into the twentieth,
after a series of mutations that are also reiterations. We are
talking about a movement that embraces all the countries of the
Western World, from Slavic to Spanish American, but that, at
each stage, is concentrated into two or three points of radiance.
Symbolism was essentially French, though this does not mean
there were no great Symbolist poets in other languages (I
hardly need mention Russian, German, or Spanish American
Symbolism). It moves from Baudelaire to Mallarmé, Verlaine,
Rimbaud, and Laforgue, and from them to Claudel and Valéry.
Avant-guard poetry is at one and the same time a reaction
against Symbolism and its continuation. The work of Guil-
laume Apollinaire, the poet who typifies this moment, shows
traces of the avant-guard and of Symbolism. The birthplace of
avant-guard poetry, France, explains its literary genealogy.
From its beginnings, the avant-guard was the contradictory
metaphor of French Symbolism.

In addition to this relationship, another non-polemical, convergent, even filial one that should be mentioned was with
contemporary painting, especially Cubism. This relationship
was neither literary nor verbal, but conceptual; poets did not

extract a language but an aesthetic out of the Cubist experience. If the avant-guard started by speaking French, it was cosmopolitan French, with Spanish, Polish, Italian, Russian, German, and Romanian accents. A language that, despite having come from Rimbaud, Mallarmé, and Jarry, conformed, deformed, and reformed itself when it encountered the new aesthetic of painters and sculptors. The new language had many names, the most convenient of which, because the most descriptive, is *simultaneísmo* (simultanism). It was a poetics that originated in Cubism and Futurism. One of Cubism's main tenets was the simultaneous presentation of the various parts of an object—seen from in front, from behind, visible, hidden—thus showing the relationships among them. Cubism conceived of the painting as a surface where the different external and internal elements of an object are unfolded, drawn in one direction then another by the forces of attraction and repulsion, complementary oppositions. To use the time-honored expression, the painting turned into a "system of plastic relationships." Jakobson has emphasized the fact that the influence of Cubist painting was as profound or more profound than that of atomic physics in orienting the thought of the first structuralist linguists. It is scarcely worth recalling the other, often invoked analogy between simultanism and cinematographic montage, especially as practiced and explicated by Sergei Eisenstein.

As we know, the Futurists added two dimensions to this intellectualist aesthetic: sensation and movement. Also its name: simultanism. They were the first to use the word and the concept. The introduction of sensation and movement produced unsuspected consequences. Sensation is movement, and from

Aristotle on, movement has been inseparable from time. Perhaps for this reason, whenever the philosophers of Antiquity tried to understand the paradox of eternity, which is time standing still, they used the circular movement of the heavenly bodies, a movement that always returns to its starting point. The twentieth century's simultanism had to face a similar difficulty: the simultaneous representation of sequentiality. When the Italian Futurists proclaimed an aesthetic of sensation, they opened the door to temporality. Time came in through the doorway of sensation, but it was fragmented, non-sequential time: the moment. Sensation is instantaneous. And so, by its very aesthetic, Futurism condemned itself, not to the constructions of the future, but to the destructions of the moment. Translating the painting of sensation and movement into the language of poetry was even more disconcerting and counterproductive. The simultanist poem—it would be more exact to call it instantanist—was no more than a juxtaposition of interjections, exclamations, and onomatopoeias. Instead of moving toward the future, the Futurist poem disappeared into the abyss of the moment, or came to a standstill in a disconnected series of fixed moments. The elimination of time as sequence and as change: the Futurist aesthetic of movement resolved itself in the abolition of movement. The agents of this petrification were sensation and the moment.

I do not know whether Apollinaire realized the negative consequences of a doctrine that in its works destroyed the very thing it exalted in its theory—movement. But it is certain that he was very aware of the poetic poverty of Futurist poems. His *Futurist Antitradition* (1913), the manifesto he published in support of it, was an act of literary opportunism. Henri-Martin Barzun also made an attempt to overcome the obstacle that gets in the way of all verbal simultanism. The obstacle is twofold: how to produce a simultaneous representation of movement, which by its nature is process, sequence, and—especially true of movement in and of itself—time? and how to organize verbal material, which is essentially temporal and successive, in a spatial, simultaneous arrangement? The solution of Barzun— founder of a "simultanist" group to which Apollinaire belonged for a short time—was even simpler than that of the Futurists. It was to turn the poem into a sort of musical drama. The model of Futurist poetry was the sounds of the modern city: *bruitism*; Barzun's was opera. The first name Barzun chose for his poetic school was "dramatism." Poems were to be heard, not read. The method's limitation was obvious: each actor had to say his part at the same time that the others were saying theirs. The limitation was really an impossibility: the poem could not be heard. Apollinaire soon abandoned Barzun's ideas and company.

The antidote to sensation and its instantaneous dispersion is reflection. Between one sensation and the next, between one moment and the one that follows, reflection interposes a distance that is also a bridge—a way of measuring. This distance is called rhythm; it is also called symbol or idea. A poem by Mallarmé or Valéry is a symbol of symbols; a Cubist painting is the idea of an object laid out as a system of relationships. In the Symbolist poem and the Cubist painting the visible reveals the invisible, but the revelation is achieved by diametrically opposed methods. In the poem, the symbol evokes without naming; in the painting, shapes and colors present without representing. Symbolism was *transposition* (Mallarmé); Cubism was *presentation*. In Apollinaire's work the passage from transposition to presentation is consummately achieved. It is possible that the poet could not have taken this decisive step without the influence of the painter Robert Delaunay and his Orphism. An offspring of Cubism, this trend was one of the manifestations of simultanism in painting. Furthermore, as its name indicates, Orphism had certain Symbolist elements—the idea of universal correspondence—and indisputable affinities with the hermeticism of abstractionism, as conceived of by Kandinsky (*Concerning the Spiritual in Art*).

The friendship between Apollinaire and Delaunay produced admirable poems like *Les fenêtres*. However, pictorial Orphism offered no solution to the problem of movement in poetry. Different colors and shapes that the eye perceives simultaneously can be presented at the same time and on the same surface. But when we speak and write we utter words one after the other, like beads on a string; not only can we not hear several phrases at the same time, but we cannot understand them if we read them. Apollinaire discovered the solution in the poetry of Blaise Cendrars. Two of Cendrars' poems made an impression on Apollinaire and inspired some of his great compositions during those years: *Pâques à New York* (1912) and *Prose du Transibérien et la petite Jeanne de France* (1913). In both of these, rather than simultanism in the pictorial Cubist sense, Cendrars uses a method of composition that is none other than narrative. An interrupted narrative, with comings and goings, anticipations, interruptions, digressions, and unforeseen twists.

Cendrars' poems are closer to film than to painting, more like montage than collage. But Cendrars could not have used this cinematographic technique if he had not used *spoken language* as a means of pulling together rhymes, images, episodes, events, and sensations. Cendrars does not sing; he narrates. Not the moment with its onomatopoeias and interjections, but everyday speech, daily language that flows and passes, this was the channel by which real time, simultaneous and discontinuous, found its way into our century's poetry. And it appeared in the very place where, since the eighteenth century, the poetic tradition has confused eloquence with poetry and has resisted the seduction of colloquial speech: France.

Apollinaire's simultanism was not of the pure variety. It could not be. Like Cendrars', it was a compromise. The poem remained a verbal structure, linear and sequential, but tending to give the sensation—or the illusion—of simultaneity. Apollinaire, more in control of his expressive resources than Cendrars, understood immediately that in poetry the suppression of syntactic connectives was an act whose consequences were analogous to the abolition of perspective in painting. His way of writing was juxtaposition. But juxtaposition is a word that cannot truly describe Apollinaire's procedure in his great poems. In each of these compositions there is a secret center, an axis of attraction and repulsion, around which stanzas and images whirl. In *Le musicien de Saint-Merry*, for example, this axis is a mythic figure that is also autobiographical. The musician is Orpheus and also the devil of a Renaissance legend, he is an automaton who reminds us of those painted by Chirico around the same time, and he is Apollinaire himself. Just as the planets arrange themselves around the sun, the juxtaposition arranges itself around this plural and singular personage. The musician is the center of the poem, a moving center. He wanders through the streets of an old district of Paris, and his music calls together different times and spaces, women living and dead, shopkeepers, Republican guards, and ghosts. It is a magnetic center. In *Zone*, a more frankly autobiographical poem than *Le musicien de Saint-Merry*, the technique is the same: the poet walks through the streets of Paris, and, like a sorrowful, living magnet, attracts to himself other times and places. Everything flows together and appears, becomes present, in a slice of motionless time that is also a slice of space in motion. This is one of the aspects of Apollinaire's art that critics have not explored but that all his readers have felt with great intensity. The present of *Zone*, *Le musicien de Saint-Merry*, *Cortège*, and other poems, confluence of all times, becomes motionless and acquires the fixity of space, while space becomes fluid, bifurcates, comes together again, and is lost. Space acquires the properties of time.

Apollinaire's poetic universe is inhabited by two hostile sisters, sympathy and antipathy, in the meaning the ancient Stoics gave these words. Conjunction and dispersion and again conjunction of times and spaces: meetings, separations, loves, deaths, hatreds: *destinies*. Apollinaire's simultanism is a variant of the old theory of correspondences, a kind of analogy in which the idea of destiny appears naturally. The religion of the stars still lives in Apollinaire. He represents one more example of the vitality of the hermetic current that has secretly nourished the poetry of the West from the Renaissance on. Apollinaire's simultanism also borders on irony. In the poem *Lundi rue Christine*, simultanism becomes the conjunction, or, more accurately, confusion of languages. The poem is a tiny box of echoes, in which snatches of conversations heard in a restaurant resonate. A criticism of human beings and of language: what we say and hear at all times is words without meaning.

Simultanist poetry—though it was not known by this name—reached its greatest purity in the work and person of Pierre Reverdy. Reverdy's mission in the realm of poetry was similar to that of Juan Gris in painting. Both represent rigor: with them and in them the avant-guard turns on itself, reflects, and, without losing its spirit of adventure, develops consciousness. Reverdy's ideas are very like those expressed around the same time by Gris, and some have pointed out the Spanish painter's influence on the French poet. It's quite likely. In any case, the prose texts Reverdy has left us, many of which were written long after Gris's death, show him to have been an original thinker—not only about aesthetics but also about moral, historical, and political issues. Reverdy's poetry and criticism show a much clearer understanding of Cubism than Apollinaire's. Influenced by this uncompromising aesthetic, Reverdy tends to turn each poem into an object. Not only does he suppress anecdote and music, narrative and song (Apollinaire's great resources), but he pushes his asceticism to extremes and almost completely eliminates connectives and relative pronouns. The poem shrinks to a series of verbal blocks with no syntactic links, joined one to another by the magnetism of the image.

Reverdy worked out a doctrine of the poetic image as autonomous spiritual reality that, in addition to influencing André

Breton and the Surrealists, affected poets as different as William Carlos Williams and Vicente Huidobro. The French poet thought of the image as the discovery of secret or hidden relationships among objects; the image will be proportionately stronger and more efficacious depending on how far apart from each other objects are and how necessary relationships between them are. The idea of an art that does not imitate reality is justified by the centrality of the image in Reverdy's poetics: the image is true reality. Within the verbal economy of the poem the image holds the place traditionally reserved for rhyme and analogy. Or more precisely: the image is the essence of analogy and rhyme, the most perfect and synthetic form of the universal correspondence. In the solar system that is each poem, the image is the sun. Thus Reverdy opened the way for Surrealism and, without knowing it, prepared the destruction of his own poetics.

Symbolism had shown scant sympathy for anecdote and for historical themes. Reverdy was even more rigorous, and, by closing the door left open by Claudel and Valéry Larbaud on the one hand and Cendrars and Apollinaire on the other, he finally expelled anecdote and biography from French poetry. The expulsion of biography culminated in the rejection of history, condemned to eternal exile. Like Cubist paintings, Reverdy's four compositions are windows, but windows that open not outward but inward. The poem is a closed space in which nothing happens, nothing takes place, not even time. A poem by Reverdy is a spiritual fact: everything that makes up the human being—sensations, feelings, other men and women—has been passed through the filter of poetry. What remain in the poem are essences. The Futurists had seen the object as sensation; Reverdy turns sensations and even feelings into objects. He immobilizes the moment—and so he salvages time. In his best poems time is alive. But it is time imprisoned, time that does not pass. Reverdy purified simultanism and, by purifying it, he sterilized it. From 1916 until his death his poetry scarcely changed. He wrote a great deal and over many years, but he always wrote the same poem. Reverdy is one of the most intense poets of this century; he is also one of the most monotonous.

Even before his early, felicitous discoveries became repetitions of a formula, Reverdy's poetry was overtaken, first by Dada and then, overwhelmingly, by Surrealism. For Reverdy the poem was a spiritual construct, possessed by its own life and detached from the reality of its origin and circumstances; for Dada, and even more so for the Surrealists, what counted was not so much the poem as poetry. For them poetry was not a construct but an experience, not something we make but something that makes and unmakes us by turn, something that happens to us: a *passion*. The final end of poetry for Reverdy was the contemplation of a verbal object, the poem, in which we recognize ourselves. Poetry as *re-cognition*. For the Surrealists poetry was not contemplation but a means of transforming the world and mankind; not a re-cognition but a metamorphosis. The principle governing the production of poems was different too; the Surrealists' answer to simultanism was the voice of the unconscious. The resurrection of inspiration destroyed the intellectualist bases of the poetics derived from Cubism and Orphism. The dictates of the unconscious replaced the simultaneous presentation of different realities and, consequently, destroyed the idea of the painting and the poem as systems of relationships made up of equivalences and oppositions. Because what inspiration dictates is linear and sequential, Surrealism reintroduced linear order. Never mind that by virtue of its content the Surrealist text subverts reason, morality, or everyday logic; the order in which this delirium reveals itself is the old syntactic order. From this point of view, Surrealism was more of a step backward.

Simultanism disappeared from France but was adopted by the American poets, especially Pound. Confirming once again the symmetrical and contradictory evolution of modern poetry in English and in French, American poets used simultanism in a way that was completely different from that of the French: not to exclude history from poetry but as the axis of the reconciliation between history and poetry. The masterpieces of Pound and Eliot were constructed using simultanist techniques. It is true that the French also produced several long poems during this period, some of them admirable. I am thinking of Saint-John Perse's vast compositions. But it is not simultanism that triumphs in them; rather they derive from the sometimes inspired, other times emphatic tradition that runs from Rimbaud's prose poems to Claudel's *Les cinq grandes odes*. At the close of this era André Breton wrote the *Ode à Charles Fourier*, in which he separates himself from Surrealist poetry and takes up historical, moral, and philosophical themes. That great poem does not use simultanism either, but returns to the intrinsically French tradition—late Hugo, Rimbaud, Perse— which at one extreme borders on prophetic inspiration and, at the other, on eloquence.

It was Pound who introduced simultanism into English. Not only in his own work but through his influence on the composition of *The Waste Land*, the first great simultanist poem in English and one of the most important poems of our century. Pound often talked about his poetics and about his method of writing the *Cantos*. Though it seems strange, he never mentioned Apollinaire nor the simultanism of the years immediately preceding the First World War. Instead he insisted on the example of Chinese poetry and claimed that the method used in the *Cantos*—the suppression of connectives and bridges, justaposition of images—was a result of his having read Ernest Fenellosa and of that famous Orientalist's interpretation of ideographic writing and the use of ideograms by Chinese and Japanese poets. J. J. Liu has shown unequivocally that Pound's and Fenellosa's ideas contain "a basic misconception." According to Liu, "The majority of the Chinese characters are Composite Phonograms (*Hsieh-Sheng*) and contain a phonetic element (the other part of the composite character, which signifies the meaning, is called the 'radical' or 'significant'). Moreover, even those characters which were originally formed on a pictographic principle have lost much of their pictorial quality, and in their modern forms bear little resemblance to the objects they are supposed to depict . . . The fallacy of Fenellosa and his followers should now be evident." It is true that another Chinese critic and poet, Wai-lin Yip, claims that the absence of syntactic connectives in Chinese poetry—his favorite example is Wang Wei—partially justifies the Fenellosa-Pound interpretation. Without denying that Yip's observation is reasonable, I find it clear and self-evident that the compositional method of the *Cantos* is already found in Apollinaire's simultanism. It is impossible for Pound not to have encountered the poems of Cendrars, Apollinaire, and Reverdy during his years in Paris. He was friendly with Picabia and collaborated in various reviews and publications of the Dada movement and other avant-guard groups, such as *Dada*, number 7 (*Dadophone*, 1920), *Littérature* (number 16. October 1920), or 391 (number 15, 1921). Consider a poem like *Lundi rue Christine*. All one has to do is change the quotations of colloquial phrases into quotations from literary, historical, and philosophical texts in several languages, and change the theme—for example, the fall of Troy superimposed on the fall of Paris or Berlin—to find the method of the *Cantos* in embryo.

Let me repeat that I do not deny the American poet's originality. Pound's great discovery—also used by Eliot in *The Waste Land*, thanks to his advice—was to apply simultanism not to Apollinaire's limited, personal and traditional themes, but to the history of the Western World. Pound's greatness, and, to a lesser degree, that of Eliot—though in the final analysis the latter seems to me a more perfect poet—lies in his attempt to reclaim the tradition of *The Divine Comedy*, that is, the main tradition of the West. Pound set himself to write the great poem of a civilization, but—*make it new!*—to do it using the procedures and discoveries of the most modern poetry. Reconciliation of tradition and avant-guard: simultanism and Dante, the *Shy-King* and Jules Laforgue.

In short, simultanism has two great moments: its origin in France, and its high noon in the English language. Similarity and contradiction: the poetic method is the same, but it is inserted into different and opposing ideas of what poetry is. And in Spanish? Vicente Huidobro picked up this trend in his early creacionist poems, brilliant but futile adaptations of Reverdy and Apollinaire. Later he abandoned them; there is no simultanism in his great poem *Altazor*. The Mexican José Juan Tablada wrote a small, perfect simultanist poem, *Noctorno Alterno*. But again, one swallow does not make summer. We had to wait for my generation for simultanism to appear in poetry as well as, very energetically, in the novel.

*

Romanticism was not only a reaction against the Neoclassical aesthetic but against the Greco-Latin tradition, as formulated by the Renaissance and the Baroque. Neoclassicism, after all, was only the last and most radical manifestation of that tradition. The return to national poetic traditions (or the invention of these traditions) was a rejection of the central tradition of the Western world. It was not fortuitous that the first expressions of Romanticism, together with the Gothic novel and medievalism, were Wathek's orientalism and the American vastness of Natchez. Cathedrals and Gothic abbeys, mezquitas, Hindu temples, deserts, American forests: signs of denial rather than images. Real or imaginary, each edifice and landscape was a polemical proposition against the tyranny of Rome and its heritage. In his essays of poetic criticism, Blanco White spends little time on the influence of French Neoclassicism because he goes straight to the heart of the matter: the source of the evil which afflicts Spanish poetry lies in the sixteenth century; its name is the Italian Renaissance. Eloquence, regularity, Petrarchism: symmetry which distorts, geometry which strangles Spanish poetry and prevents it from being itself. To recover their own being, Spanish poets must free themselves from that heritage and return to their real tradition. Blanco White does not say what that tradition is, except that it is *other*. A different tradition from that worshiped in equal measure by Garcilaso, Góngora, and the Neoclassical poets. The main tradition of Europe is turned into an aberration, a strange imposition. It had been the unifying element—the bridge between languages, spirits, and nations: now it is alien. Romanticism obeys the same centrifugal impulse as does Protestantism. If it is not a schism, it is a separation, a breach.

The breaking of the main Western tradition caused many traditions to appear; this plurality of traditions led to the acceptance of different ideas of beauty; aesthetic relativism became the justification of the aesthetic of change—the critical tradition which affirms itself in its very self-denial. Within this tradition, Anglo-American poetic modernism is a great change, a great rejection, and a great novelty. The breach consists in that, far from being a rejection of the main tradition, it is a search for it. Not a revolt, but a restoration. A change of direction: reunion, not separation. Although Eliot and Pound held different ideas about what this tradition really was, their starting point was the same: consciousness of the schism, the feeling and the knowledge of being cut off. A double schism, both personal and historical. They went to Europe not as expatriates, but in search of their origins; their journey was not one of exile but a return to the source. It was a movement in the opposite direction from Whitman's: not the exploration of unknown spaces, the American beyond, but the return to England. However, England, separated from Europe since the Reformation, was only one link in the broken chain. Eliot's

Anglicism was a European trait; Pound, more of an extremist, jumped from England to France and from France to Italy.

The word "center" appears frequently in the writings of both these poets, generally in association with the word "order." Tradition becomes identified with the idea of a center of universal convergence, an earthly and a heavenly order. Poetry is the search for, and sometimes the vision of, this order. For Eliot the historical image of spiritual order is medieval Christian society. The idea of the modern world as the disintegration of Christian order in the Middle Ages appears in many writers of this period, but in Eliot it is more than an idea, it is a destiny and a vision. Something thought and lived—something spoken: a language. If the modern era is for Eliot the breaking up of Christian order, his individual fate as poet and modern man has its place precisely in this historical context. In its turn, history turns toward the spiritual sphere. Modern history is fall, separation, disintegration; it is likewise the way of purgation and reconciliation. Exile is not exile: it is the return to timeless time. Christianity takes time upon itself only to transmute it. Eliot's poetics become transformed into a religious vision of modern Western history.

In Pound's case the idea of tradition is more confused and changeable. Confused, because it is not so much an idea as a juxtaposition of images; changeable, because, like the Griffin Dante saw in Purgatory, it changes endlessly while remaining always the same. There lies perhaps his profound Americanism: his search for the central tradition is only one more form, the extreme, of the tradition of search and exploration. His involuntary resemblance to Whitman is surprising. Both of them go beyond the bounds of the Occident, but one searches for a mystical-pantheistic effusion (India), the other for a wisdom which will bring the heavenly order into harmony with that of the earth (China). Pound's fascination with Confucius' system is like that of the eighteenth-century Jesuits and, like theirs, is a political passion. The Jesuits thought a Christian China would be a world model; Pound dreamed of a Confucianized United States.

The extraordinary richness and complexity of the references, allusions, and echoes of other epochs and civilizations make the *Cantos* a cosmopolitan text, a true poetic babel (and there is nothing pejorative in this designation). Nevertheless, the *Cantos* are primarily a North American poem written for North Americans—which obviously does not prevent them from fascinating everyone. The various episodes, figures, and texts present in the poem are models which the poet proposes to his compatriots. All are aimed toward a universal or, to more exact, imperial, standard. In this Pound differs from Whitman. One sings of a national society, broad as a world, which would finally bring about democracy; the other of a universal nation, heir to all civilizations and all empires. Pound talks about the world but thinks always about his country, a world-wide country. The nationalism of Whitman was a universalism; the universalism of Pound a nationalism. This is the reason for the Pound cult of the political and moral system of Confucianism: he saw in the Chinese Empire a model for the United States. From this too his admiration for Mussolini. The ghost of Justinian of the final *Cantos* corresponds also to this imperial vision.

The center of the world is not the place where the religious word is manifest, as in Eliot; it is the source of energy that moves men and joins them in a common cause. Pound's order is hierarchical although his hierarchies are not based on money. His passion was neither liberty nor equality but grandeur and justice among unequals. His nostalgia for the agrarian society was not nostalgia for the democratic village but for the old imperial societies such as China and Byzantium, two great bureaucratic empires. His mistake consisted not in his vision of those civilizations but, rather, in not recognizing the enormous weight of the state, crushing the peasants, artisans, and merchants. His anticapitalism, as can be seen in the famous *Canto* against Usury, expresses a legitimate horror toward the modern world, but his condemnation of money-grubbing is that of the medieval Catholic Church. Pound did not recognize that capitalism is not usury, it is not the hoarding of excremental gold, but rather its sublimation and transformation through human effort into social products. The usurer's hoarding stems wealth, retires it from circulation, while the products of capitalism are in turn productive: they circulate and multiply. Pound ignored Adam Smith, Ricardo, and Marx—the ABC of the economy and of our world.

Pound's excremental obsession is associated with his hatred of usury and with antisemitism; the other face of that obsession is his solar cult. Excrement is demoniac and terrestrial; its image, gold, is hidden in the bowels of the earth and in the coffers, symbolic bowels, of the usurer. But there is another image of excrement which is its transfiguration: the sun. The excremental gold of the usurer is hidden in the depths; the sun lights the heights for all. Two antithetical movements: excrement returns to the earth; the sun extends above it. Pound admirably perceived the opposition between these two images but he did not see the connection, the contradictory relation uniting them. In all imperial emblems and visions the sun or its homolog—the solar bird, the eagle—occupies the central position. The emperor is the sun. In the celestial order—the rotation of the planets and the seasons round a luminous axis—this is the way to govern the earth. Order, rhythm, dance: social harmony, justice from those on high, loyalty from those below. Pound's dream is, like that of Fourier though in an opposite sense, an analogy of the solar system.

For Eliot poetry is the vision of divine order seen from here, from a world cast adrift from history; for Pound it is the instantaneous perception of the fusion of the natural (divine) order with the human order. Instants become archetypal: the hero's feats, the lawgiver's code, the emperor's scales, the artist's creation, and, above all, the apparition of the goddess, "with the veil of faint cloud before her / Κυθηρα δεινά as a leaf borne in the current." History is hell, purgatory, heaven, limbo—and poetry is the tale, the story of man's journey through these worlds of history. Not only the story, also the objective presentation of moments of order and disorder. Poetry is *paideia*. Those instantaneous visions that rend the shadows of history as Diana the clouds, are not ideas or things—they are light. "All things that are are lights." But Pound is not a contemplative; these lights are acts and they suggest a course of action.

The search for the central tradition was a reconnoitering expedition, in the military sense of the expression: a polemic and a discovery. A polemic because it saw the history of English poetry as a gradual separation from the central tradition. Chaucer, says Pound in the *ABC of Reading*, participates in the intellectual life of the continent and is a European, but Shakespeare "is already looking back to Europe from the outside." A discovery in that it finds those works which actually belong to the central tradition and shows the bonds which unite them. European poetry is an animated and coherent whole. Pound wonders: "Can anyone estimate Donne's best poems save in relation with Cavalcanti?" Eliot in turn uncovers affinities between the "metaphysical" poets and some French Symbolists, and between both of these and the Florentine poets of the thirteenth century. This reconstruction of a tradition extending from the Provençal poets to Baudelaire was an assembly not of ghosts but of living works. In the center is Dante, the standard, the touchstone. Eliot reads Baudelaire from Dante's perspective, and *Les fleurs du mal* turns into a modern commentary on the *Inferno* and the *Purgatorio*. Wedged between the *Odyssey* and the *Divine Comedy*, Pound writes an epic poem which is also a hell, a purgatory, and a paradise. The *Divine Comedy* is an allegorical rather than an epic poem; the poet's journey through the three worlds is an allegory of the *Book of Exodus*, in turn an allegory of the history of the human race from the Fall to the Last Judgment, which is only an allegory of the wanderings of the human soul, redeemed at last by divine love. Its theme is the return of the soul to God; the theme of the *Cantos* is also a return, but to where? In the course of the journey the poet has forgotten his destination. The matter of the *Cantos* is epic; the tripartite division is theological. Secularized theology: authoritarian politics. Pound's fascism, before being a moral error, was a literary error, a confusion of genres.

The bringing together of the fragments was not an antiquarian labor, but a rite of expiation and reconciliation: the purging of the sins of Protestantism and Romanticism. The results were contradictory. In his expedition to reconquer the central tradition, Pound went beyond Rome—to China six centuries before Christ—while Eliot stayed at the halfway point, the Anglican Church. Pound discovered not one but many traditions and embraced them all; along with plurality he chose juxtaposition and syncretism. Eliot chose only one tradition, but his vision was no less eccentric. Eccentricity was not a mistake on the part of these two poets; it was embodied in the very origin of the movement and in its contradictory nature. Anglo-American "modernism" conceived of itself as a "classical revival." It is with precisely this expression that T. E. Hulme opened his essay "Romanticism and Classicism." The young English poet and critic had found an aesthetic and a political credo in the ideas of Charles Maurras and his movement *L'Action Française*. Hulme pointed out the connection between Romanticism and revolution: "it was Romanticism that made the Revolution." This is oversimplification: the initial affinity between Romanticism and revolution resolved itself, as we have seen, in opposition. Romanticism was an anti-rationalism; the revolutionary Terror scandalized the Romantics precisely because of its systematic nature and its rational pretensions. In his reply to Madame de Staël, "On Germany," Heine pointed out that Robespierre had cut off the heads of the nobility with the same logic with which Kant had decapitated the ideas of the old metaphysics. Although Hulme criticized the aesthetic ideas of the German Romantics, his attitude and that of his circle recalled the spirit of the Romantics. In both, hatred of the revolution became nostalgia for the medieval Christian world. This is an idea which appears in all the German Romantics and which Novalis formulated in his essay "Europe and Christianity." The new Christian society, born out of the ruins of rationalistic, revolutionary Europe, would finally realize the union foreshadowed by the Holy Roman Empire. The Classicism of Hulme, Eliot, and Pound was a Romanticism which did not recognize itself as such.

Maurras' movement claimed to be the heir of the Greco-Roman and medieval tradition: Classicism, rationalism, monarchism, Catholicism. It is scarcely worth noting that this tradition is dualistic and contradictory from its origins: Heraclitus/Parmenides, monarchy/democracy. Moreover, the Reformation, Romanticism, and the Revolution now have become the central stream, and that which Eliot and his friends wished to restore has become marginal. In the history of modern France, Maurras' movement was that of a political faction. Not only was it marginal historically speaking, it was also heretical in a religious sense: Rome condemned it. Maurras' rationalism did not exclude the cult of authority nor the suppression of criticism by violence and antisemitism. His poetical classicism was an archaism. In his political ideas the cardinal concept was that of the nation: a Romantic idea. In search of the central tradition, Eliot pursued a sect which was schismatic in religion and marginal in aesthetics. Who reads Maurras' poems today? Fortunately, the anti-Romanticism of Hulme, Eliot, and Pound was less strict than that of Maurras. Less strict and less coherent. They invented a poetic tradition featuring the very names the Romantics had claimed as their own. The most notable were Dante and Shakespeare. Both had been used as weapons against the Neoclassical aesthetic and the hegemony of Racine. The inclusion of the "metaphysical" poets—the English expression of European Baroque poetry and "conceptismo"—did not fall into line with what is generally understood by Classicism. Hulme graciously justified these violations of Classicist orthodoxy: "that Racine is on the extreme classical side, I agree . . . but Shakespeare is the classic of motion." Clever but not convincing.

While Anglo-American "modernism" was finding inspiration in Maurras, the young French poets were discovering Lautréamont and Sade. There could be no greater difference. European avant-garde movements were tinged with a strong Romantic coloration, from the most timid, like German Expressionism, to the most exalted, like the Futurisms of Italy and Russia. Dada and Surrealism were ultra-Romantic, though it is almost redundant to say so. The extreme formalism of some of these trends—Cubism, constructivism, abstractionism—seems to belie my claim. But it does not: the formalism of modern art is a rejection of the naturalism and humanism of the Greco-Roman tradition. Its historical origins are outside the Classical tradition of the West: black art, pre-Colombian art, the art of Oceania. Formalism continues and accentuates the trend begun by Romanticism: to oppose other traditions to the Greco-Roman tradition. Modern formalism destroys the idea of representation—in the sense of Greco-Roman and Renaissance illusionism—and submits the human figure to the stylization of a rational or passional geometry—when it does not expel it from the picture altogether. It is said that Cubism was a reaction against the Romanticism of the Impressionists and Fauves. This is true, but Cubism is only intelligible within the contradictory context of the avant-garde, in the same way that Ingres is only *visible* when faced with Delacroix. In the history of the avant-garde, Cubism is the moment of reason not of Classicism. A delirious reason, suspended over the abyss, between the Fauves and the Surrealists. As for the geometries of Kandinsky and Mondrian: they are impregnated with occultism and hermeticism, so that they prolong the deepest and most persistent current of the Romantic tradition. The European avant-garde, even in its most rigorous and rational manifestations—Cubism and abstractionism—continued and exacerbated the Romantic tradition. Its Romanticism was contradictory, a critical passion which ceaselessly denies itself in order to regenerate itself.

Oppositions repeat, though conversely, those of the Romantic period: Pound condemns Góngora exactly when the young Spanish poets proclaim him their master; for Breton the Celtic myths and the Grail legend bear witness to the *other* tradition— the tradition which denies Rome and which was never completely Christian—while for Eliot these same myths acquire spiritual meaning only when they come into contact with Roman Christianity; Pound sees in Provençal poetry a Poetics and the beginning of our tradition, the Surrealists see in it a subversive erotic tradition—subversive in the face of bourgeois morality because of its exaltation of adultery, and subversive

in the face of modern promiscuity for its celebration of exclusive love; the European avant-garde exalts the aesthetic of
the exception, Eliot wants to reintegrate the religious exception—the Protestant separation—into the Christian order of
Rome, and Pound tries to insert within a universal order the
historical peculiarity which is the United States; Dada and
the Surrealists destroy the codes of law, and heap sarcasm and
spittle upon altars and institutions, Eliot believes in the Church
and the Monarchy, Pound proposes for the United States the
image of Leader-Philosopher-Savior, a mixture of Confucius,
Malatesta, and Mussolini; for the European avant-garde the ideal
society is outside history—it is the world of the primitives or
the city of the future, the dateless past or the communistic and
libertarian utopia—while the archetypes Eliot and Pound offer
are empires and churches, historical models; Dada denies the
works of the past and those of the present as well, and the
Anglo-American poets insist upon the reconstruction of a
tradition; for Surrealism the poet writes that which his unconscious dictates to him, poetry is the transcription of the *other*
voice which speaks in each of us when we quiet the voice of
wakefulness, while for the Anglo-Americans poetry is technique,
control, mastery, consciousness, lucidity; Breton was a friend
of Trotsky and Eliot a monarchist. The list of oppositions
is endless. Even in political and moral "errors" the symmetry
of opposition reappears: Pound's Fascism is balanced by the
Stalinism of Aragon and Neruda.

The Surrealists believe in the subversive power of desire and
in the revolutionary function of eroticism. The Spaniard
Cernuda sees in pleasure not only a physical explosion but a

moral and political criticism of Christian and bourgeois
society:

Abajo estatuas anónimas,
Preceptos de niebla:
Una chispa de aquellos placeres
Brilla en la hora vengativa.
Su fulgor puede destruir vuestro mundo.

(Down with anonymous statues, / Rules of fog: / A spark of
those forbidden pleasures / Glitters in the vengeful hour.
/ Its flash can destroy your world.) The different evaluations of
dreams and visions are no less striking than those of eroticism.
Eliot remarked that Dante "lived in an age in which men still
saw visions . . . We have nothing but dreams and we have
forgotten that seeing visions was once a more significant,
interesting and disciplined kind of dreaming. We take for
granted that our dreams spring from below: possibly the quality
of our dreams suffers in consequence." The Surrealists exalted
dreams and visions but refused to distinguish between them:
both spring from below, both are revelations of the abyss—the
"other side" of men and reality.

All these oppositions can be absorbed in one: the European
avant-garde breaks with all traditions and thus continues the
Romantic tradition; the Anglo-American movement breaks
with the Romantic tradition. Contrary to Surrealism, it is an
attempt at restoration rather than a revolution. Protestantism
and Romanticism had separated the Anglo-Saxon world from
the religious and aesthetic tradition of Europe: Anglo-American

"modernism" is a return to this tradition. A return? I have
already indicated its involuntary resemblance to German
Romanticism. Its denial of Romanticism was also Romantic:
the reinterpretation of Dante and the Provençal poets by
Pound and Eliot was no less eccentric than the reading of
Calderón by the German Romantics a century earlier. The position of the terms is inverted but the terms do not disappear,
nor does the relationship between them. Anglo-American
"modernism" is *another* version of the European avant-garde,
just as French Symbolism and Spanish American "modernismo"
had been other versions of Romanticism. Versions: metaphors:
transmutations.

   The Anglo-American "restoration" was no less profound and
radical a change than was the Surrealist "revolution." This
observation is applicable not only to the *Cantos* and *The Waste
Land* but also to the poetry of Wallace Stevens, e. e. cummings,
and William Carlos Williams. I have referred almost exclusively
to Pound and Eliot because there is in both of them a critical
and programmatic facet which does not appear in other poets of
this generation. Apart from this, I do not believe that those
poets are less important than Pound and Eliot. But "important"
is a foolish word: each poet is different, unique, irreplaceable.
Poetry cannot be measured; it is neither small nor great—it
is simply poetry. Without the verbal explosions of cummings,
resulting from his extreme and admirable poetic concentration;
without the transparency and density of Wallace Stevens'
"Esthétique du mal" and "Notes Toward a Supreme Fiction,"
poems in which, as in "The Prelude," the gaze of the poet
(now disenchanted and freed from romantic and avant-garde

mirages) traces a bridge between "the mind and the sky"; without the poems of Williams, who, as Stevens said, gave us "a new knowledge of reality"—modern Anglo-American poetry would be greatly impoverished. And we also. Anglo-American cosmopolitanism started as a radical formalism. It is precisely this formalism—poetic *collages* in Pound and Eliot, verbal transgressions and combinations in cummings and Stevens—which links Anglo-Saxon modernism to the European and Latin American avant-gardes. Although it pro-. claimed itself an anti-Romantic reaction, Anglo-American formalism was nothing but another manifestation of the duality which has been present in modern poetry from its inception: analogy and irony. Pound's poetic system consists of presenting images as clusters of signs upon the page: ideograms, not static but moving, like a landscape seen from a ship or, rather, like constellations moving toward or away from each other on the surface of the sky. The word "constellation" calls forth the idea of music; and the word "music," with its innumerable associations from the erotic harmony of bodies to political harmony among men, conjures up the name of Mallarmé. Here is the heart of analogy. Pound is not a disciple of Mallarmé, but the best part of his work belongs in the tradition begun by *Un coup de dés*. In the *Cantos* as in *The Waste Land* analogy is continuously torn apart by criticism, by ironic consciousness. Mallarmé and Duchamp: analogy ceases to be a vision and turns into a system of permutations. Like the erotic-industrial, mythic-ironic duality of the *Large Glass*, all the characters in *The Waste Land* are real and mythic. Reversibility of signs and significances: in Duchamp, Artemis is a "pin-up," and in Eliot the image of heaven and its rotating constellations turns into a deck of cards spread out on a table by a fortune-teller. The image of cards leads to that of dice, and the latter once again to the image of the constellations. In the mirror of the empty room described in the "Sonnet en ix," Mallarmé sees the seven stars of the Great Bear reflected like seven notes which "relient au ciel seul ce logis abandonné du monde." In *Arcane 17* (once again Tarot and the magic of the cards), André Breton looks from the window of his room and sees the night doubly night, earthly night echoed by the night of twentieth-century history, until gradually the black square of the window, like Mallarmé's mirror, is lit up and an image is outlined: "seven flowers which turn into seven stars." The rotation of signs is really a spiral, in whose curves appear, disappear, and reappear, alternately masked and naked, the two sisters—analogy and irony. An anonymous collective poem of which each of us is a stanza, a handful of syllables, rather than author or reader.

There is a curious similarity between the history of modern poetry in Spanish and in English. At almost the same time Anglo-American and Spanish American poets left their native lands; they absorbed new trends in Europe, transforming and changing them; they leapt over two formidable obstacles (the Pyrenees and the English Channel); they burst onto the scene in Madrid and London, awakening the drowsy Spanish and English poets; their innovators (Pound and Huidobro) were accused of Gallican and cosmopolitan heresies; contact with the new trends led two great poets of the previous generation (Yeats and Jiménez) to doff their Symbolist robes and write their best poems near the end of their lives; the initial cosmopolitanism soon produced negation: the Americanism of Williams and of Vallejo. The oscillations between cosmopolitanism and Americanism display our dual temptation, our common mirage: the land we left behind, Europe, and the land we seek, America. The similarity between the evolution of Anglo-American and Spanish American literature results from the fact that both are written in transplanted languages. Between ourselves and the American soil a void opened up which we had to fill with strange words. Indians and mestizos included, our language is European. The history of our literatures is the history of our relations with the place that is America, and also with the place where the words we speak were born and came of age. In the beginning our letters were a reflection of European ones. However, in the seventeenth century a singular variety of baroque poetry was born in Spanish America that was not only the exaggeration but at times the transgression of the Spanish model. The first great American poet was a woman, Sor Juana Inés de la Cruz. Her poem *El Sueño* (1692) was our first cosmopolitan text; like Pound and Borges later, the Mexican nun built a text as a tower—again, Tower of Babel. As another example of her cosmopolitanism, in other poems the Mexican note appears together with a mixture of languages: Latin, Castilian, Nahúatl, Portuguese, Indian, mestizo, and mulatto dialects. Sor Juana's Americanism, like that of Borges, is a cosmopolitanism; this breed of cosmopolitanism also expresses a Mexican and Argentinian mode of existence. If it occurs to Sor Juana to speak of pyramids, she cites those of Egypt, not of Teotihuacán; if she writes an *auto sacramental* such as *El divino*

Narciso, the pagan world is personified not by a Greek or Latin divinity but by the pre-Colombian god of the harvests.

The strain between cosmopolitanism and Americanism, between cultured and colloquial language, is constant in Spanish American poetry from the time of Sor Juana Inés de la Cruz. Among the Spanish American *modernistas* at the end of the last century, cosmopolitanism was the dominant tendency in the early phase of the movement, but, as I have shown, the reaction toward colloquialism, critical and ironic (the so-called "post-modernismo"), sprang from the heart of the movement itself. Around 1915 Spanish American poetry became characterized by regionalism, love for conversational speech, and ironic view of the world and of man. When Lugones speaks of the corner barber, this barber is no symbol but a being marvelous just because he is the corner barber. López Velarde extolls the power of a mustard seed, affirming that his voice is "la gemela de la canela" (twin of the cinnamon). In Spain, Spanish American colloquialism was transformed into the reconquest of the rich vein of traditional poetry, both medieval and modern. In Antonio Machado and Juan Ramón Jiménez the aesthetic (and the ethic) of the immense smallness also predominated: universes fit into a couplet. Some young men followed other paths: a symbolism endowed with a classical consciousness (more or less inspired by Valéry), as, for instance, Alfonso Reyes in his *Ifigenia cruel* (1924); or a poetry stripped of everything picturesque, like that of Jorge Guillén. But the extreme alternative was the appearance of a new cosmopolitanism, no longer bound up with Symbolism, but with the French avant-garde of Apollinaire and Reverdy. As in 1885, the initiator was a Spanish

American: at the end of 1916 the young Chilean poet Vicente Huidobro arrived in Paris; soon afterward, in 1918 in Madrid, he published *Ecuatorial* and *Poemas Articos*. With them the Spanish avant-garde commenced.

Huidobro was worshiped and reviled. His poetry and his ideas inspired many young poets, and two movements were born from his example, the Spanish and the Argentinian "ultraísmo"—both angrily rejected by the poet as imitations of his "creacionismo." Huidobro's ideas are undeniably similar to those which Reverdy was then expounding: the poet does not copy reality, he produces it. Huidobro affirmed that the poet imitates not nature but its *modus operandi*: he makes poetry as the rain and the earth make trees. Williams said something similar in the prose pieces interspersed in the first edition of *Spring and All* (1923): the poet produces poetic objects as electricity produces light. But Huidobro resembles cummings rather than Williams. Both are descendants of Apollinaire, both are lyrical and erotic, both scandalized with their syntactic and typographic innovations. cummings is more concentrated and perfect; Huidobro more vast. His language was international (that is one of his limitations), and more visual than spoken. Not a language of earth but of aerial space. An aviator's language: the words are parachutes which open in midair. Before touching earth they burst and are dissolved in colored explosions. Huidobro's great poem is *Altazor* (1931): the hawk assaulting the heights and disappearing, burned up by the sun. Words lose their meaningful weight and become not signs but traces of an astral catastrophe. The Romantic myth of Lucifer reappears in the form of the aviator-poet.

Spanish American avant-garde and Anglo-American "modernism" were as much transgressions of the canons of London and Madrid as flights from American provincialism. In both movements oriental poetry, especially haiku, exercised a beneficent influence. The poet who introduced haiku into Castilian was José Juan Tablada, who also wrote ideographic and simultaneist poems. But these are formal similarities. Opposed cosmopolitanisms: what Pound and Eliot sought in Europe was the exact opposite of what Huidobro, Oliverio Girondo, and the Borges of those years were seeking. Anglo-American modernism sought to return to Dante and to Provence; the Spanish Americans proposed to carry to its extremes their revolt against that tradition. Accordingly, Huidobro never denied Darío: his "creacionismo" was not the rejection of modernismo but its *non plus ultra*.

In the beginning Spanish American avant-garde depended on the French, as before the first modernistas had followed the Parnassians and Symbolists. The revolt against the new cosmopolitanism again assumed the form of nativism or Americanism. César Vallejo's first book (*Los heraldos negros*, 1918) extended the poetic line of Lugones. In his second book (*Trilce*, 1922) this Peruvian poet assimilated the international forms of the avant-garde, internalizing them. A true translation, or rather, transmutation. Huidobro's opposite number: poetry of the earth, not of the air. Not of any earth: one history, one tongue. Peru: men/stones/dates. Indian and Spanish signs. The language of *Trilce* could only be that of a Peruvian, but of a Peruvian who was also a poet who saw the man within each Peruvian, and the witness and victim within each man. Vallejo was a great religious poet. A militant Communist, the background of his vision of the world and of his beliefs was not the critical philosophy of Marxism but the basic mysteries of the Christianity of his childhood and of his race: communion, transubstantiation, longing for immortality. His verbal inventions impress us not only because of their extraordinary concentration but for their authenticity. Sometimes we stumble over his failures of expression, awkwardnesses, stammers. It does not matter: even his least successful poems are alive.

Nativism and Americanism appear in many poets of this period. For instance, in the Borges of *Fervor de Buenos Aires* (1923), which contains a series of admirable poems dedicated to death and to the dead. In the United States, too, reaction to Eliot's cosmopolitanism broke out, a reaction represented principally by Williams and "objectivists" like Louis Zukofsky and George Oppen. The similarity, once again, is formal. The Anglo-Americans, faced with the landscape of the industrial age, interested themselves above all in the object—its geometry, its internal and external relations, its meaning—and felt scarcely any nostalgia for the pre-industrial world. In the Spanish Americans this nostalgia was an essential element. Industry does not appear in the Anglo-Americans as a theme but as a context. Propertius' modernity consists not in the theme of the great city but in the fact that the great city appears in his poems without the poet's having expressly intended it: the same is true of Williams. On the other hand, some Spanish American poets, Carlos Pellicer and Jorge Carrera Andrade, use terms and metaphors of the modern world to depict the American landscape: aviation and Virgil. It is revealing that in

Pellicer's poetry pre-Colombian ruins occupy the same favored place as the magic of the industrial object in a Zukofsky poem.

Recapitulation of the episodes of modernismo: Spanish American colloquialism and nativism were transformed in Spain into traditionalism—the ballads and songs of Federico García Lorca and Rafael Alberti. The influence of Juan Ramón Jiménez was decisive in orienting the young Spanish poetry. However, in 1927, the three hundredth anniversary of Góngora's death, the direction changed. The rehabilitation of Góngora was initiated by Rubén Darío, and studies by various eminent critics followed. But the resurrection of the great Andalusian poet results from two circumstances: the first is that among the critics was a poet, Dámaso Alonso; the second, decisive factor is the coincidence which the young Spaniards noticed between Góngora's aesthetic and that of the avant-garde. In his *Antología poética en honor de Góngora* (Madrid, 1927), the poet Gerardo Diego emphasizes that the important thing is to create verbal objects (poems) "made of words only," words "which should be more like spells than verses." The aesthetic of Reverdy and of Huidobro. The same Gerardo Diego later published a memorable poem, *Fábula de Equis y Zeda* (1932), in which baroque elements are combined with *creacionismo*. In the minds of Spanish poets the formalism of the avant-garde was associated with Góngora's formalism. Nor is it strange that during these years José Ortega y Gasset should publish *La deshumanización del arte*.

Two poets resisted both traditionalism and neo-Gongorism: Pedro Salinas and Jorge Guillén. The former composed a kind of lyrical monologue in which the things of modern life—movies, automobiles, telephones, radiators—are reflected in the clear waters of an eroticism which stems from Provence. Guillén's work, as I once wrote, "is an island and a bridge." An island, since in the face of the upheaval of the avant-garde Guillén had the incredible insolence to say that perfection is also revolutionary; a bridge, because "from the beginning Guillén was a master, as much for his contemporaries (García Lorca) as for those of us who came later."

A new breach: the parasurrealist explosion. In English-speaking countries the influence of Surrealism was belated and superficial (until the appearance of Frank O'Hara and John Ashbery, in the fifties). On the contrary, it was early and very profound in Spain and Spanish America. I say "influence" because, although there were artists and poets who participated individually in different periods of Surrealism—Picabia, Buñuel, Dali, Miró, Matta, Lam, César Moro, and I myself—neither in Spain nor in America was there Surrealist activity in the strict sense. (An exception: the Chilean group *Mandrágora*, founded in 1936 by Braulio Arenas, Gonzalo Rojas, Enrique Gómez-Correa, and others.) Many poets of that period adopted onirism and other surrealist procedures, but it cannot be claimed that Neruda, Alberti, or Aleixandre were Surrealists, despite the fact that in certain moments of their work, their searches and discoveries coincided with those of the Surrealists. In 1933 a book by Pablo Neruda, *Residencia en la tierra*, appeared in Madrid. An essential book. Huidobro's poetry evokes the element of air; Vallejo's, that of the soil; Neruda's, of the water. Ocean more than lake. Neruda's influence was like a flood which spreads and covers miles and miles—confused, powerful, somnambulant, shapeless waters. Those years saw a wealth of production: *Poeta en Nueva York* (1929), probably Federico García Lorca's best book, containing some of the most intense poems of this century, such as the "Oda a Walt Whitman"; Vicente Aleixandre's *La destrucción o el amor* (1935), a vision of erotic passion at once dark and sumptuous; *Sermones y moradas* (1930) of Rafael Alberti—a subversion of the language of religion which starts to rave and puts bombs on altars and in confessionals; *Nocturnos* (1933) of Xavier Villaurrutia, which contains six or seven of the best poems of the decade—metallic, brilliant, anguished poetry, the dual voice of desire and sterility; Ricardo Molinari, whose strange high noon contains trees with no shade; Luis Cernuda, he who most brilliantly and courageously accepts the duality of the word *pleasure*—active criticism of social morality and the door leading to death. The Spanish Civil War and World War II put an end to this period. The Spanish poets were dispersed and the Spanish Americans isolated.

Many of these poets moved from individual revolt to social revolt. Some joined the Communist Party, others the cultural organizations which the Stalinists had created in the shadow of the Popular Fronts. The result was the manipulation of many generous impulses—though one cannot discount a contemptible dose of opportunism—by Communist bureaucracies. Poets acquired "socialist realism" and practiced the poetry of social and political propaganda. The verbal search and the poetic adventure were sacrificed on the altars of clarity and political efficacy. A large part of those poems have disappeared as the columns and editorials of newspapers disappeared. They sought to bear witness to history, and history has obliterated them. The most serious thing was not the lack of poetic but of moral tension: the hymns and odes to Stalin, Molotov, Mao—and the more or less rhymed insults to Trotsky, Tito, and other dissidents. A curious realism which forced its authors to contradict themselves after Khrushchev's revelations. Yesterday's truths are today's lies: where is reality? That was the era of the "poets' dishonor," as Benjamin Péret called it.

Even those who refused to place their art at the service of a party almost completely renounced poetic experimentation and invention. There was a general retreat to order. Political didacticism and neoclassical rhetoric. The old avant-gardists— Borges, Villaurrutia—devoted themselves to writing sonnets and *décimas*. Two books representative of the best and the worst of this period are the *Canto general* (1950) of Pablo Neruda, and José Gorostiza's *Muerte sin fin* (1939). The former is enormous, disjointed, confused, though interspersed here and there by passages of great materialist poetry: tide-language and lava-language. The other is a poem of some eight hundred blank verses, a discourse in which intellectual consciousness bends the flow of language until it freezes it into a hard transparency: rhetoric and great poetry. Two extremes: the passionate yes and the reflective no. A monument to loquacity and a monument to reticence.

About 1945 poetry in our language divided into two academies; that of "socialist realism" and that of the repentant avant-garde. The change was initiated by a few books from a scattering of poets. Here ends all pretension to objectivity: even if I wanted to, I could not dissociate myself from this period.

I shall therefore try to reduce it to a few essential points. It all begins with a book by José Lezama Lima, *La fijeza* (1944). Then, in 1949 (I cannot avoid mentioning it) I published *Libertad bajo palabra* and in 1951 ¿*Aguila o sol?* At almost the same time, in Buenos Aires, appeared Enrique Molina's *Costumbres errantes o la redondez de la tierra* (1951). A little later, Nicanor Parra, Alberto Girri, Jaime Sabines, Cintio Vitier, Roberto Juarroz . . . These names and these books are *not* all of contemporary Spanish American poetry; they are its beginning. To speak of what has followed, important though it is, would mean to write a chronicle.

The beginning: a clandestine, almost invisible action. At first almost nobody paid attention to it. In a certain sense it marked the return of the avant-garde. But a silent, secretive, disillusioned avant-garde. An *other* avant-garde, self-critical and engaged in solitary rebellion against the academy which the first avant-garde had become. It was not a question of inventing, as in 1920, but of exploring. The territory which attracted these poets was neither outside nor inside. It was the zone where external and internal merge: the zone of language. Theirs was not an aesthetic preoccupation; for these young men language was, simultaneously and contradictorily, their destiny and their choice. Something given and something we make—and which makes us.

Language is the man but also the world. It is history and biography: others and myself. The new poets had learned to reflect and to make fun of themselves: they knew that the poet is the tool of language. They also knew that the world did not begin with them, but they did not know whether it would end

with them: they had lived through Nazism, Stalinism, and the
atomic explosions in Japan. Their lack of communication with
Spain was almost total, not only because of the political
circumstances but because the postwar Spanish poets lingered in
the rhetoric of social or religious poetry. They were attracted
by Surrealism, a waning movement, and considered the post-
modernist Anglo-American poets—Lowell, Olson, Bishop,
Ginsberg—as their true contemporaries, even if (or because) the
Anglo-Americans were emerging from the opposite side of the
modern tradition. They also discovered the poetry of Pessoa, and
through it the work of the Brazilian and Portuguese poets of
their generation, such as Cabral de Melo. Although some of them
were Catholics and others Communists, they leaned toward
individualistic dissidence, oscillating between Trotskyism and
anarchism. But it would be absurd to put ideological tags
on them. In the face of world events they felt horror for
Western civilization and, at the same time, attraction for the
East, the primitives, or pre-Columbian America. Theirs was a
sort of religious atheism, a religious rebellion against religion. It
was more a search for an Erotica than for a new Poetics. Almost
all identified themselves with Camus' words from those second
postwar days: "solitaire solidaire." It was a generation which
accepted marginality and made of it their true homeland.
Post-avant-garde poetry (I don't know if we must resign ourselves to this name, which some critics are beginning to give us)
was born as a silent rebellion of isolated men. It started as an
insensible change which, ten years later, showed itself to be
irreversible. Between cosmopolitanism and Americanism, my
generation made a clean and permanent break: we are con-

demned to be Americans as our fathers and grandfathers were condemned to seek America or flee from her. Our leap has been within ourselves.

The Twilight of the Avant-Garde

Opposition of the modern age works within the age. To criticize it is one of the functions of the modern spirit; and even more, one way of fulfilling it. The modern age is the age of schism and of self-negation, the age of criticism. It has identified itself with change, change with criticism, and both with progress. Modern art is modern because it is critical. Its criticism unfolded in two contradictory directions: it rejected the linear time of the modern age and it rejected itself. By the first it denied modernity; by the second affirmed it. Faced with history and its changes, it postulated the timeless time of the origins, the moment, or the cycle; faced with its own tradition, it postulated change and criticism. Each artistic movement rejected its predecessor, and through each of these rejections art perpetuated itself. Only within linear time can rejection develop to the full, and only in a critical age like ours can criticism be creative. Today we witness another mutation: modern art is beginning to lose its powers of negation. For some years now its rejections have been ritual repetitions: rebellion has turned into procedure, criticism into rhetoric, transgression into ceremony. Negation is no longer creative. I am not saying that we are living the end of art: we are living the end of the *idea of modern art*.

Art and poetry are inseparable from our earthly destiny: art existed as soon as man became man and will exist until man disappears. But our ideas as to what art is, from the magic vision of the primitives to the *Manifestes* of Surrealism, are as many and as diverse as are societies and civilizations. The decline of the tradition against itself manifests the general crisis of the modern era. I have dealt with this theme in some of my writings; here I will confine myself to a brief enumeration of the most obvious symptoms. In the first two chapters I showed that our idea of time is the result of a critical process: the destruction of Christian eternity was followed by the secularization of its values and its transposition into another category of time. The modern age begins with the revolt of the future. Within the perspective of medieval Christianity the future was mortal: the Last Judgment was to be the day of its abolition and the advent of an eternal present. The critical process of the modern age inverted the terms: the only eternity known to man was that of the future. For the medieval Christian earthly life came to rest in the everlasting existence of either good or bad; for modern man it is an endless march toward the future. That is where the height of perfection lies, not in an eternal life beyond death. Now, in the second half of the twentieth century, certain signs indicate a change in our system of beliefs. The conception of history as a progressive and linear process has been proved inconsistent. That belief was born with the modern age, and, to a certain extent, has been its *raison d'être*. The loosening of its hold reveals a fissure in the very heart of the contemporary consciousness: the modern era is beginning to lose faith in itself.

The belief in history as a continuous march, notwithstanding some stumbles and falls, took many forms. Sometimes it was a naive application of Darwinism to the realms of history and society; at other times it was a vision of the historical process as the progressive realization of freedom, justice, reason, or some other similar value. In yet other cases history came to be identified with the development of science and technology or with man's dominion over Nature or with the universalization of culture. All these ideas have something in common: it is man's destiny to colonize the future. In recent years there has been a sharp change: people begin to look fearfully toward the future, and what only yesterday seemed the marvels of progress have become its disasters. The future is no longer the storehouse of perfection but of horror. Demographers, ecologists, sociologists, physicists, and geneticists are denouncing the march toward the future as a march toward destruction. Some foresee the exhaustion of natural resources, others the contamination of the earth itself, others an atomic flare-up. The achievements of progress are called hunger, toxic poisoning, volatilization. I am not concerned here as to whether or not these prophecies are exaggerated: I want to emphasize that they are expressions of a general doubt about progress. It is significant that in a country like the United States, where the word "change" has enjoyed a superstitious reverence, another has appeared which refutes it utterly: "conservation." The present has become critical of the future and is beginning to displace it.

Marxism was probably the most coherent and most daring expression of history as a progressive and linear process. The most coherent because it conceives of history as a process with the rigor of rational discourse; the most daring because the discourse embraces the past and present as well as the future of the human race. Science and prophecy. For Marx history is a single process—the same for all mankind—that unfolds like a mathematical series or logical proposition. Each proposition generates an apposition resolved in an affirmation. In this way, through negations and contradictions, new stages are evolved. History is like a text which begets other texts. It is a process which moves from the communism of primitive society to that of the industrial era. The protagonists of this process are the social classes, propelled by the force of different productive techniques. Each historical period marks an advance on the preceding one, and in each period one social class takes upon itself the representation of all humanity: feudal aristocracy, bourgeoisie, proletariat. The latter embodies the historical present and its immediate future. I repeat what we all know: if the violent changes of the twentieth century confirm Marx's apocalyptic vision, the form in which they have come about denies the supposed rationality of the historical process.

The absence of proletarian revolutions in more industrially advanced countries, like the revolts on the fringes of the Western world, show that Marxist ideology has not fomented the workers' world revolution nor real socialism but only the national resurrection of Russia, China, and other countries slow to reach the age of industry and technology. The protagonists of these changes were not the workers, but classes and groups which Marxist theory placed at the edge or in the rear of the historical process: intellectuals, peasants, lower middle class. More serious still: the revolutions which triumphed have been transformed into regimes which are anomalous from a strict Marxist point of view. It is a historical aberration that socialism should take on the form of dictatorship by a new bureaucratic class or caste. The aberration disappears if we give up the conception of history as a progressive, linear process blessed with an immanent rationality. It is hard to resign ourselves to this because giving up this belief implies the end of our claims to shape the future. Nevertheless, it is not a renunciation of socialism as ethical and political *free choice*, but of the idea of socialism as a *necessary product* of the historical process. Criticism of the political and moral aberrations of contemporary "socialisms" should begin with criticism of our intellectual aberrations. History is not single: it is plural; it is the history of men and of the marvelous diversity of societies and civilizations which men have created. Our future, our idea of the future, totters and hesitates: the plurality of pasts makes plausible the idea of a plurality of futures.

The revolts in underdeveloped countries and on the fringe of industrialized societies belie the previsions of revolutionary thought; the rebellions and disorders in the more advanced countries undermine even more thoroughly the idea of the future which evolutionists, liberals, and progressive bourgeois had made for themselves. It is remarkable that the class to which the revolutionary vocation per se was attributed has not shared in the disturbances which have shaken the industrialized societies. Recently an attempt has been made to explain this phenomenon by a new social category: the more advanced societies, especially the United States, have now passed from the industrial to the postindustrial age. The latter is characterized by the importance given to what could be called the production of productive knowledge, in other words, a new mode of production in which knowledge occupies the central position hitherto held by industry. Social struggles in the postindustrial society are not the result of the opposition between labor and capital, but conflicts in the cultural, religious, and psychic spheres. Thus, the student disorders of the last decade can be seen as an instinctive rebellion against the excessive rationalization of social and individual life demanded by this new mode of production. Different modes of dehumanization: capitalism treated men like machines; the postindustrial society treats them like signs.

Whatever value there may or may not be in lucubrations on the postindustrial society, the fact is that, despite their just and passionate rejection of the present state of things, rebellions in developed countries do not offer programs for the organization of the society of the future. For this reason I call them rebellions, not revolutions. This indifference toward the shape the future should take distinguishes the new radicalism from the revolutionary movements of the nineteenth century and the first half of the twentieth. Confidence in the strength of spontaneity exists in inverse proportion to the disgust toward systematic constructs. The discrediting of the future with its geometric paradises is widespread. Nor is this strange: in the name of building the future half of the planet has been covered with forced labor camps. The rebellion of youth is a movement of rejection of the present, but it is not an attempt to build a new society. The young people want to end the present situation precisely because it is a present which oppresses us in the name of a chimerical future. They have the instinctive but confused hope that the destruction of this present will bring about the sudden appearance of the *other* present with its corporal, intuitive, and magical values. Always that search for the *other time*, the real time.

In rebellions of ethnic and cultural minorities, demands for economic redistribution are not the only, nor often the central, issues. Blacks and Chicanos are struggling for recognition of their identity. Something similar is taking place with women's liberation movements and even with those of sexual minorities: it is not so much a question of erecting the city of the future as of the emergence, within contemporary society, of groups searching for identity or struggling for recognition. Nor do the nationalist and anti-imperialist movements, wars of liberation, and other disturbances of the Third World fit into the idea of revolution worked out by the linear and progressive conception of history. These movements are the expression of particularisms which were humiliated during the period of Western expansion, and for this reason they have become models for the struggles of ethnic minorities in the United States and elsewhere. The revolts in the Third World and the rebellions of ethnic and national minorities in industrialized societies are the uprisings of particularisms oppressed by another particularism wearing the mask of universality: Western capitalism. Marxism foresaw the disappearance of the proletariat as a class immediately after the disappearance of the bourgeoisie; the dissolution of classes corresponded to the universalization of mankind. Contemporary movements tend in the opposite direction: they are affirmations of each group's individuality, and even of sexual idiosyncrasies. Marxism postulated a future in which all classes and peculiarities would dissolve in one universal society; today's struggle is for recognition here and now of the concrete and individual reality of each and every one.

All these rebellions appear as a breach in the idea of linear time. They are the irruption of the offended present and thus, explicitly or implicitly, postulate a devaluation of the future. The background for these rebellions is the changed sensibility of the age. Decay of the Protestant and Capitalist ethic with its moral code of savings and work: two ways of shaping the future, two attempts to get the future into our power. The insurrection of corporal and orgiastic values is a rebellion against man's twofold penalty—condemnation to work and repression of desire. For Christianity the human body was *fallen Nature*, but divine grace could transfigure it into the *glorious body*. Capitalism deconsecrated the body; it ceased to be a battlefield for angels and devils and became a work tool. The conception of the body as a tool led to its degradation as a source of pleasure. Asceticism changed; instead of a means to get to heaven, it became a technique to increase productivity. Pleasure is a waste, sensuality an embarrassment. To condemn pleasure was to condemn the imagination because the body is not only a wellspring of sensations but of images. The disorders of the imagination are no less prejudicial to production and optimum output than physical shudders of sensual pleasure. In the name of the future the censure of the body culminated in the mutilation of man's poetic powers. Nowadays the rebellion of the body is also that of the imagination. Both reject linear time: their values are those of the present. The body and the imagination do not know the future; sensations are the abolition of time in the instantaneous moment, the images of desire dissolve past and future in a timeless present. It is the return to the beginning of the beginning, to the sensibility and passion of the Romantics. The resurrection of the body may be an omen that man will eventually recover his lost wisdom. The body not only rejects the future: it is a path toward the present, toward that here and now where life and death are two halves of one and the same sphere.

These various signs signal a change in our image of time. At the beginning of the modern era, Christian eternity lost its ontological reality as well as its logical coherence; it became a senseless proposition, an empty word. Today, the future seems no less unreal than eternity. From Hume to Marx, criticism of religion by philosophy is applicable to the future: it is not real and it robs us of reality; it does not exist and it robs us of life. Yet the critique of the future has been made not by philosophy but by the body and by the imagination.

The Ancients overesteemed the past. To confront its tyranny, man invented an ethic and an aesthetic of exceptions based on the instant. Against the rigors of the past and of precedents, he opposed the freedom of the instant: neither a before nor an after but a now—the time-out-of-time of pleasure, religious revelation, or poetic vision. In the modern age the instant also has been a barrier to domination by the future. In opposition to historical time, successive and infinite, modern poetry since Blake has affirmed the time of origin, the moment of the beginning. The time of origin is not a before, it is a now. It is a reconciliation of the beginning and of the end; every now is a beginning and every now is an end. The return to the beginning is a return to the present.

The vision of the present as a point of convergence of all times, originally a vision of poets, has become the underlying belief in the attitudes and ideas of most of our contemporaries.

The present has become the central value of the temporal triad. The relation between the three times has changed, but this does not imply the disappearance of the past or of the future. On the contrary, they gain more reality: they become dimensions of the present, both are present—both are presences in the now. The time has come to build an Ethics and a Politics upon the Poetics of the now. Politics ceases to be a construction of the future; its mission is to make the present habitable. The ethics of now is not hedonistic in the ordinary sense of the word, although it affirms both pleasure and the senses. The present reveals that the end is neither different from nor opposed to the beginning, but its complement, its inseparable half. To live in the present is to live facing death. Man invented eternity and the future to escape death, but each of these inventions was a fatal trap. The present reconciles us with reality: we are mortal. Only facing death, life is really life. Within the now, death is not separated from life. Both are the same reality, the same fruit.

The end of the modern era, the fall of the future, can be seen in art and in poetry as an acceleration which dissolves the notion of future as well as that of change. The future instantly becomes the past; changes are so swift that they produce the sensation of immobility. The *idea* of change was the cornerstone of modern poetry, rather than the changes themselves: today's art must differ from yesterday's. Now, to perceive the difference between yesterday and today there must be a certain rhythm. If changes come about very slowly they run the risk of being confused with immobility. This was what happened with the art of the past: neither artists nor public, hypnotized by the idea of "imitation of the ancients," could perceive changes with clarity. We cannot perceive them today, but for the opposite reason: they disappear as rapidly as they appear. Actually they are not changes; they are variations of earlier models. Imitation of the moderns has sterilized more talents than imitation of the ancients. We must add proliferation to false speed: not only do avant-garde movements die almost as soon as they are born, but they spread like weeds. Diversity is resolved in uniformity. The fragmentation of the avant-garde into hundreds of identical movements: in the anthill differences disappear.

Romanticism brought the mixture of genres. Symbolism and the avant-garde completed the fusion of prose and poetry. The results were marvelous monsters, from Rimbaud's prose poem to Joyce's verbal epic. The mixture and ultimate abolition of genres culminated in the criticism of the art object. The crisis of the idea of oeuvre became apparent in all the arts— painting, sculpture, poetry, the novel—but its most radical expression was Duchamp's "ready-mades." Derisive consecration: what counts is not the object but the artist's act in separating it from its context and placing it on the pedestal of the old work of art. The gesture takes the place of the work. In China and Japan many artists, on discovering a certain aesthetic irradiation in an anonymous stone, would pick it up and sign their name to it. This gesture was one of recognition rather than discovery. It was a ceremony which paid homage to Nature as a creative force: Nature creates and the artist recognizes. The context of Duchamp's "ready-mades" is not creative Nature but industrial technology. His gesture is not an act of choice or of recognition but of rejection; in an atmosphere of non-choice and of indifference, Duchamp finds the "ready-made," and his gesture is the dissolution of recognition in the anonymity of the object. His gesture is an act of criticism, not of art, but of *art as object*. Since the days of Romanticism modern poetry had been critical of the subject. Our age has perfected this criticism. The Surrealists granted a primordial function in poetic creation to the unconscious and to chance; now some poets emphasize ideas of permutation and combination. In 1970, for example, four poets (a Frenchman, an Italian, an Englishman, and a Mexican) decided to compose a collective poem in four languages (which they called by the Japanese name *Renga*). Not only a combination of different texts but of producers of texts (poets). The poet is not the "author" in the traditional sense of the word; he is a moment of convergence of the different voices which flow into a text. Criticism of the object and of the subject intersect in our time: the art object dissolves in the instantaneous act, the subject is a somewhat fortuitous crystallization of language.

The end of art and poetry? No: the end of the "modern era" and, with it, the end of the idea of "modern art and literature." Criticism of the object prepares the way for the resurrection of the work of art, not as something to be possessed, but as a presence to be contemplated. The work is not an end in itself nor does it exist in its own right: the work is a bridge, an intermediary. Nor does criticism of the subject imply the destruction of poet or artist but only of the bourgeois idea of author. For the Romantics, the voice of the poet was the voice of *all*; for us

it is the voice of *no one*. "All" and "no one" are equal to
each other, and both are equally far from the author and his
"I." The poet is not a "little god," as Huidobro wanted. The
poet disappears behind his own voice, a voice which is his
because it is the voice of language, the voice of no one and of
all. Whatever name we give this voice—inspiration, the unconscious, chance, accident, revelation—it is always the voice of
otherness.

   The aesthetic of change is no less illusory than that of imitation of the Ancients. One tends to minimize changes, the other
to exaggerate them. The history of the poetic revolutions
of the modern age has been none other than the dialogue
between analogy and irony. The former rejected the modern
age; the latter, analogy. Modern poetry has been criticism
of the modern world and criticism of itself. Criticism which
resolves itself in poems, from Hölderlin to Mallarmé. Poetry
builds transparent monuments out of its own fall. But irony and
analogy, the image and the bizarre are only moments in the
rotation of signs. The dangers of the aesthetic of change are also
its virtues: if everything changes, the aesthetic of change also
changes. This is what is happening today. Modern poets looked
for the principle of change; poets of the dawning age look for
the unalterable principle that is the root of change. We wonder
if the *Odyssey* and *A la recherche du temps perdu* have anything
in common. This question, more than denying the avant-garde,
is a question which extends beyond it. The aesthetic of change
accentuated the historical nature of the poem. Now we ask: is
there a point where the principle of change blends into that of
permanence?

The historical character of the poem is immediately evident by virtue of its being a text which someone has written and someone else reads. The writing and reading of the poem are acts that happen; they take place in time and can be dated. They are history. But, from another perspective, the contrary is also true. While he is writing, the poet does not know what his poem will be like; he will know only when he reads it, after it is finished. The author is the poem's first reader, and with his reading a series of interpretations and re-creations begins. Each reading produces a different poem. No reading is definitive, and in this sense each reading, not excluding that of the author, is an accident of the text. The text dominates its author-reader and its subsequent readers. It remains and resists the changes of each reading. The text resists history. At the same time, the text comes into being only through those changes. The poem is a trans-historical potentiality actualized in history, in the reading. There is no poem *in itself*, only *in me* or *in you*. Fluctuation between the trans-historical and the historical: without a text there is no reading, and without a reading there is no text. The text is the condition of the readings, and the readings realize the text, insert it in the sequence of time. The relation between the text and its readings is *contradictory* and *necessary*.

A poem is a text but at the same time it is a structure. The text rests on the structure—its support. The text is visible, legible; the skeleton is invisible. All novels have similar structures, but *Madame Bovary* and *The Turn of the Screw* are two unique, unmistakable texts. The same is true of epic poems, sonnets, or fables. The structure of the *Odyssey* resembles that

of the *Aeneid*: both obey the same laws of rhetoric, yet each
one is a different, irreplaceable text. Each poetic text actualizes
certain structures common to all poems—and each text is an
exception to and often a violation of these structures. The
texts vary, the structures are constant. Literature is a kingdom
in which each work is unique. Baudelaire fascinates us precisely
with what is his alone and not found in either Racine or
Mallarmé. In science we seek recurrences and similarities—laws
and systems; in literature, exceptions and surprises—unique
works. A science of literature such as that claimed by some
French structuralists (certainly not Jakobson) would be a
science of particular objects. A non-science: a catalogue or
ideal system ceaselessly belied by the reality of each work.

The structure is ahistoric; the text is history, it bears a date.
From the structure to the text and from the text to the reading:
the dialectic of change and of identity. The structure is invariable in relation to the text, but the text is constant in relation
to the reading. The text is always the same—and at each reading
it is different. Each reading is a dated experience which denies
history by virtue of the text and which by reason of this denial
forces itself again within history. Variation and repetition: the
reading is an interpretation, a variation of the text, and in that
variation the text is realized, is repeated—and absorbs the
variation. Finally, the reading is historical and, at the same time,
is the dissipation of history in an undated present. The date
of the reading melts away; the reading is a repetition (a creative
variation) of the original act: the poem's composition. The
reading returns us to another time, that of the poem. A time
that is not of calendars and clocks—a time which exists before
them.

The time of the poem is inside history, not outside it. Text and readings are inseparable, and in them history and ahistory, change and identity, are united without being dissolved. It is not a transcendence but a convergence. It is time which repeats itself and is unrepeatable, which flows without flowing: a time which turns back upon itself. The time of the reading is here-and-now: a now which happens at any moment, and a here which exists anywhere. The poem is history and it is that something which rejects history in the very instant of affirming it. To read a non-poetic text is to understand it, to capture its meaning; to read a poetic text is to resuscitate it, to *re-pro-duce* it. This *re-production* unfolds itself in history, but opens out toward a present which is the abolition of history. The poetry starting up in this second half of the century is not really starting. Nor is it returning to the point of departure. The poetry beginning now, without beginning, is looking for the intersection of times, the point of convergence. It asserts that poetry is the present, between the cluttered past and the uninhabited future. The re-production is a presentation. Pure time: heartbeat of the presence in the moment of its appearance/disappearance.

Notes

1.

The criticism of time was only one of the ways to exorcise
history. The other was the caste system. Although the Portuguese word *casta* translates fairly faithfully the term generally
used in India, *jeti*, Westerners tend to give it a meaning tinged
with historicism: implying not lineage or generation but
stratified class. The word *class* immediately links us with
history and change. From the point of view of Western anthro-
pologists and their Indian disciples, the phenomenon of caste
is but an extreme case of a universal phenomenon: the tendency
toward social stratification. This interpretation dissolves, spirits
away the unique quality of the caste concept. For there is
something specific in the idea of caste which is not found in
that of class. If we want to understand the underlying ideology
on which the reality of the castes is based, what this concept
really means for a traditional Indian, the first thing we must do
is distinguish "caste" from "class."

For us, society is a collection of classes, generally at war with
each other and all in motion. Human society forms a dynamic
whole which is continually changing; this ceaseless movement
is what distinguishes it from the social structures of animals,

which are static. In human society something appears which does not exist in nature: culture. And culture is history. The Indian conception is the contrary. There is no opposition between nature and society, the first is the archetype of the second. For an Indian the "castes"—there are more than three thousand of them—are not "classes" but species. The word "jeti" literally means species. The Indian sees human society in the immovable mirror of Nature and her unchanging species. Far from being an exception, the human world prolongs and confirms the natural order. We, used to seeing society as a process, think of the caste system as a scandalous exception, an historical anomaly. And so, the opposition between "caste" and "class" hides an even deeper contrast: between history and nature, change and stability. If men from other civilizations could mediate in the debate, they would probably say that the true exception is not the caste system—although some might recognize it as a more or less iniquitous exaggeration—nor the idea which inspires it, but our own view, which sees change as inherent in society and regards it as almost always beneficent. The unique and bizarre thing is the point of view which over-values change, converts it into a philosophy, and then makes this philosophy the foundation of society. A primitive would consider such an outlook imprudent at the very least. It all but opens the door to original chaos.

2.

After writing these pages I received an interesting study written by Edmund L. King and entitled "What is Spanish

Romanticism?" (*Studies in Romanticism*, Vol. 2, no. 1, Autumn 1962). The first part of Professor King's analysis coincides with my own: the feebleness of the Romantic reaction is explained by the poverty of Spanish Neoclassicism and by the absence of an authentic Enlightenment in Spain. However, I do not share the point of view expounded in the second half of his study, where he states that *Krausismo* was the real Spanish Romanticism, "infusing a generation of young Spaniards with genuinely Romantic concerns that would inevitably be expressed in the arts and letters of what we call the Generation of 1898." My disagreements can be summarized in two arguments.

First, Krausismo was a philosophy, not a poetic movement. There are no "Krausist" poets, although some poets at the beginning of the century (Jiménez among others) were more or less affected by the ideas of Krause's Spanish disciples.

Second, Professor King's explanation is self-contradictory, for he denies (or forgets) in the second part of his study what he affirms in the first. First he maintains that Spanish Romanticism failed because it lacked historical authenticity (although the Spanish Romantics were individually sincere); it constituted a reaction against something which Spain had not had, namely, the Enlightenment and its rationalistic criticism of traditional beliefs and institutions. In his second part he states that the Krausismo of the second half of the nineteenth century was the Romanticism Spain had lacked in the first half. Well now, if Romanticism is a *reaction* to and against the Enlightenment, Krausismo must be also a reaction—against what? He does not tell us. To clarify my point: if Krausismo is the Spanish equivalent of Romanticism, what is the Spanish equivalent of the

Enlightenment? The problem is solved if, instead of thinking of the Spanish tradition as one (the peninsular), we recognize that it is dual (the Spanish and the Spanish American). The reply to this apparent enigma lies in two words and in their contradictory relationship in the context of Spanish America: Positivism and modernismo. Positivism is the Spanish American equivalent of the European Enlightenment, and modernismo was our Romantic reaction. Of course it was not the original Romanticism of 1800, but its metaphor. The terms of this metaphor are the same as those of the Romantics and Symbolists: analogy and irony. Spanish poets of that era replied to the Spanish American stimulus in the same way that the Spanish Americans had replied to the stimulus of French poetry. Creative replies, sometimes retorts: transmutations. The links of the chain: Spanish American Positivism → Spanish American modernismo → Spanish poetry.

Why was the influence of Spanish American poetry so fruitful? Well, because, thanks to the metric and verbal renovations of the modernistas, it became possible for the first time to say things in Castilian which until then had been said only in English, French, and German. Unamuno guessed this, but only to disprove it. In a letter to Rubén Darío he said: "What I see, in you specifically, is a writer who wants to say, in Castilian, things which have never even been thought in Castilian, and which *even now* cannot be thought in our language." Unamuno regarded the modernistas as Frenchified savages who worshipped brilliant and empty forms. But there are no empty or insignificant forms. Poetic forms *say*, and the modernista forms said something hitherto unsaid in Castilian: analogy and irony. I repeat: Spanish American modernismo was the version, the metaphor, of European Romanticism and Symbolism. From this version onward, Spanish poets explored other poetic worlds for themselves.

How can one explain the minimal penetration of the ideas of the Enlightenment into Spain? In *Liberales y Románticos*, Lloréns quotes some disheartened words of Alcalá Galiano: "Without any doubt this renovation of poetry and criticism (Romanticism) was extremely salutory; but its weakness in Spain was the same as that of the doctrines erroneously called Classical, namely, that it was a foreign plant brought to our soil and transplanted in an unintelligent way which resulted in forced fruits, poor in quality, dull in color, and weak in strength." Alcalá Galiano's explanation is not convincing: sixteenth-century Italian poetry was no less strange a plant than Neoclassicism in the eighteenth century and Romanticism in the nineteenth, but its fruits were neither meager nor poor. Llorens quotes the opinion of one of the extremists or Jacobins exiled in London, who concealed his identity under the pseudonym *Filópatro*. In 1825, Filópatro wrote in *El Español constitucional*, which was considered the spokesman of the exiled extremists: "Spaniards began to enlighten themselves in secret, eagerly absorbing the choicest works of philosophy and public law of which until then they had not had the least idea . . . However, this same enlightenment (Locke, Voltaire, Montesquieu, Rousseau, and company . . .), being undigested, and totally out of contact with empirical reality, came to produce fruits more bitter even than ignorance itself." Filópatro was right: in order for the Enlightenment to have fertilized Spain it would have needed to insert ideas (criticism) into life (praxis). Spain lacked a class, a national bourgeoisie, capable of criticizing traditional society and modernizing the country.

3.

Eighteenth-century religious criticism embraced heaven and earth; it was criticism of Christian divinity, its saints and devils, criticism of its churches and priests. It criticized religion on the one hand as revealed truth and immutable scripture; on the other as a man-made institution. Philosophy undermined the conceptual edifice of theology, and attacked the church's claims to hegemony and universality. It destroyed the image of the Christian god, not the idea of God. Philosophy was anti-Christian and deist; God ceased to be a person and was converted into a concept. Confronted by the spectacle of the universe, the philosophers waxed enthusiastic: they believed they had discovered in its movements a secret order, a hidden inspiration which could only be divine. Double perfection: the universe was moved by a rational design which was also a moral design. Natural religion replaced revealed religion, and the *philosophes* replaced the Council of Cardinals. The idea of order and the idea of causality were visible manifestations, rational and sensible proofs of the existence of a divine plan; the movement of the universe was inspired by an end and a purpose: God is invisible, not his works or the intention which animates them. The materialists and atheists with very few exceptions shared this belief: the universe is an intelligent order endowed with an evident purpose, even though we do not know its final outcome.

David Hume was the first to criticize the critics of religion; his criticism remains unsurpassed and is applicable to many contemporary beliefs. In his *Dialogues Concerning Natural Religion* he showed that the philosophers had placed upon the empty altars of Christianity other divinities no less chimerical, deified concepts such as universal harmony and the purpose animating this harmony. The idea of design or purpose is the root of the religious idea; wherever it appears, not excluding atheistic and materialistic philosophies, religion also appears, and sooner or later a church, a myth, and an inquisition. The content of each religion may vary—the number of gods and ideas men have worshiped and do worship is almost infinite— but behind all these beliefs we find the same pattern: a purpose is attributed to the universe, and immediately thereafter this purpose is identified with goodness, freedom, holiness, eternity, or some similar idea.

It is not difficult to deduce from Hume's criticism the following consequence: the origin of the idea of history as progress is religious and the idea itself is para-religious. It is the result of a double and defective inference: the belief that Nature has a design, and the identification of this design with the forward motion of history and society. The same line of reasoning appears in all religions and pseudo-religions. In its first phase, as the real or apparent regularity of the natural processes is observed, the idea of finality is introduced into the order of Nature; immediately thereafter social changes and disturbances are attributed to the action of the same principle by which Nature is animated. If history really possesses a meaning, the passage of time becomes providential, though the name of this providence changes with the changes of the society and the culture: sometimes it is called God, other times evolution, and at others the dialectic of history. The importance of the calendar in ancient China (or in Mesoamerica) is another consequence of the same idea: the model of historical time is nature's time, heavenly time.

Religion is an interpretation of the original condition of man, cast into a strange world toward which his first sensation is one of abandonment, orphanhood, defenselessness. We can judge the meaning and value of religious interpretation in many ways. For example, we can say, paradoxically, that it is an act of unconscious hypocrisy, by means of which we deceive ourselves before deceiving our peers. Or we can say that it is a means of knowing or, rather, of penetrating the *other* reality, that region which we never see with our eyes open. We can also say that perhaps it is no more than the manifestation of a tendency inherent in human nature. If this were so, we would have no other recourse than to accept the existence of a "religious instinct." Hume's criticism is decisive because, by showing that inevitably we are dealing with the same operation—whatever the society, epoch, content, and nature of the representations and beliefs—he implicitly allows us to suspect that we are confronted by a mental structure common to all men. At the same time, by emphasizing its unconscious nature, he points out that it is the result of a psychic, to a certain extent instinctive, need. Hume's criticism was to be completed a century and a half later by Freud and Heidegger, but we still lack a complete description of the "religious instinct."

Whatever its origin, religion is present in all societies: in the primitive and the great societies of antiquity, in the bosom of peoples who believe in magic, and in the industrial societies of today, among the worshipers of Mohammed and those who swear by Marx. In all places and epochs the "religious instinct" turns ideas into beliefs, and beliefs into rituals and myths. It would be unfair to forget that we owe it the incarnation of ideas in perceptible images. There is nothing lovelier than the twelfth-century statue in the Indian province of Orissa representing Prajna Paramita, the Buddhist Supreme Wisdom, central metaphysical concept of the Mahayana Buddhists, as a naked, bejeweled girl. Religion's two faces: solitary experience of the mystics and the brutalizing of the populace, spiritual illumination and rapacity of clerics, communal feast and burning of heretics.

Hume's criticism can be applied to all philosophies and ideologies which are nothing more than shamefaced religions, without gods but with priests, holy books, councils, devotees, executioners, heretics, and reprobates. Hume anticipated what would follow: reason worshiped as a goddess, and the supreme being of the philosophers converted into the Jehovah of pedantic and bloodthirsty sects. Criticism of religion replaced Christianity, and in its place men hastened to enthrone a new deity: politics. The "religious instinct" depended on the complicity of philosophy. The philosophers substituted one belief for another: revealed religion for natural religion, grace for reason. Philosophy profaned heaven but consecrated earth; the consecration of historic time was the consecration of change in its most intense and immediate form: political action. Philosophy ceased to be theory and descended to men. Its incarnation was called revolution. If human history is the history of disparity and inequity, the redemption of history, the eucharist which changes it into equality and freedom is revolution.

The mythical theme of original time is converted to the revolutionary theme of future society. From the end of the eighteenth century and notably since the French Revolution, revolutionary political philosophy confiscates one by one the concepts, values, and images that traditionally belonged to religions. This process of appropriation grows keener in the twentieth century, the century of political religions as the sixteenth and seventeenth were the centuries of religious wars. For two hundred years we have lived, first the Europeans and then everyone, in the expectation of an event which will have for us the gravity and terrible fascination the Second Coming of Christ had for the early Christians: Revolution. This event, viewed with hope by some and horror by others, possesses, as I have said, a double meaning: it is the establishment of a new society and the restoration of the original society, before the days of private property, the State, scripture, the idea of God, slavery, and the oppression of women. An expression of critical reason, the Revolution places itself within historic time; it replaces the evil present with the just and liberated future. This change is a return—to the time of the beginning, to original innocence. Thus the Revolution is an idea and an image, a concept which shares in the properties of myth and a myth which is founded on the authority of reason.

In former societies, religions had two exclusive functions: to change time, and to change man. Calendar changes were not revolutionary but religious. Change of era, change of god:

the changes of the world were the changes of the other-world. Revolts, uprisings, usurptions, abdications, the advent of new dynasties, social transformations, mutations of the property system or the juridical structure, inventions, discoveries, wars, conquests—all this vast and incoherent rumble of history with its ceaseless viccisitudes did not bring about any alteration of the image of time and of the counting of years. I do not know whether one singular fact has been noted or considered: for the Mexican Indians the Conquest was a change of calendars. A change of divinities, a change of religion. In the modern world, revolution displaces religion and therefore the French revolutionaries tried to change the calendar. According to Marx's well-known dictum, the mission of the philosopher consists not so much in interpreting the world as in changing it; this change implies the adoption of a new temporal archtype: a change of Christian eternity for the future of revolutions. The religious function which consists of the creation and change of the calendar is thus transformed into a revolutionary function.

Something similar happens with the other function of religions: changing man. Ceremonies of initiation and rites of passage consist of a true transmutation of human nature. All these rituals have one thing in common: the sacrament is the symbolic bridge over which the neophyte passes from the profane to the sacred world, from this shore to the other. A crossing which is death and resurrection: a new man emerges from the ritual. Baptism changes us, gives us a name and makes us other; communion is also a transmutation, and the same is true of the viaticum—a word more meaningful than most. The central ritual in all religions is that of entry into the community of the faithful, and in every case this ritual implies a change of nature. *Conversion* expresses very clearly this mutation which is also a return to the original community. Since the birth of the modern era, and more insistently during the last fifty years, ruling revolutionaries have proclaimed that the ultimate goal of revolution is to change man: the conversion of the individual and the community. At times this claim has taken on forms which would have been grotesque had they not been atrocious, as when, combining superstition toward technology and ideological superstition, Stalin was called "engineer of men." Stalin's example is a terrifying one; others stir us deeply: Saint-Just, Trotsky. Even if moved by the Promethean nature of their pretensions, I can only deplore their ingenuity and condemn their excess.

Sources and Credits

14-15   Augustine, *The City of God.*

16   Dante, *Inferno,* canto vi.

17   "The Travels of Mirza Abū Tāleb," *Sources of Indian Tradition* (New York, Columbia University Press, 1958).

21   Dante, *Inferno,* canto x.

34   *The Everlasting Gospel, The Complete Poetry of William Blake* (New York, Random House, 1941).

39   Friedrich Hölderlin, *Poems and Fragments,* Michael Hamburger trans. (London, Routledge and Kegan Paul, 1966); *Oeuvres* (Paris, Bibliothèque de la Pléiade, 1967).

41, 44   *Letters of Percy Bysshe Shelley,* ed. F. L. Jones (2 vols., Oxford, 1964). Wordsworth, *The Prelude* (1805 text), book x, 515-516, 535-536.

46-47   Jean Paul Richter, *Siebenkäs,* 1796.

49   Nerval, *Oeuvres* (Paris, Bibliothèque de la Pléide, 1952).

53   Coleridge, "Poetry and Religion," *The Portable Coleridge,* ed. I. A. Richards (New York, Viking, 1958). Novalis, *Fragments.* Blake, "Proverbs of Hell," *The Marriage of Heaven and Hell* (1790).

54   "The Voice of the Devil," *ibid.*

56   "All Religions Are One."

58   Schlegel, *Gespräch über die Poesie* ed. H. Eichmer (1968).

62   Blake, "On Homer's Poetry and on Virgil" (1820).

68   Charles Fourier, *Théorie des quatre mouvements et des destinées générales* (Paris, Anthropos, 1967).

70-71   Charles Baudelaire, *L'art romantique*, *Oeuvres* (Paris, Bibliothèque de la Pléiade, 1941).

74   Baudelaire, "Correspondances," translated by Carlyle F. MacIntyre, *French Symbolist Poetry* (Berkeley, University of California Press, 1961).

75   Canto 83, xxxiii, 11. 86-91; translated by Dorothy Sayers, *The Comedy of Dante Alighieri the Florentine* (3 vols., Hammondsworth, Penguin, 1965-1972).

76-77   Mallarmé, *Oeuvres complètes* (Paris, Bibliothèque de la Pléiade, 1956), and *Correspondance* (2 vols., Paris, Gallimard, 1959).

79-80   Vicente Lloréns, *Liberales y románticos* (2nd ed., Madrid, 1968), and Juan Goytisolo, *Antología de José María Blanco White* in *Libre* (no. 2, Paris, 1971).

84-85   Unlike other Spanish American writers, the Argentinians sought inspiration directly from French models. Although its romanticism was also external and declamatory, the Argentinian movement a little later, and in the guise of regionalism, produced the only great Spanish American poem of this period, *Martín Fierro*, by José Hernández (1834-1866).

90   Baudelaire, "La peinture de la vie moderne" (1863), *Curiosités Esthétiques*.

92   Paz, *The Other Mexico: Critique of the Pyramid*, trans. Lysander Kemp (New York, Grove, 1972).

93   Lectures from 1940-1941. *Literary Currents in Hispanic America* (Cambridge, Mass., Harvard University Press, 1945).

94-95   Breton, *Arcane 17 enté d'ajours* (Paris, Sagittaire, 1947).

95   Darío, Poema XIII, *Otros poemas*, part 3 of *Cantos de vida y esperanza* (1905).

96-98   Lugones, *Los crepúsculos del jardín* (Buenos Aires, 1905); López Velarde, *Obras* (Mexico, F.C.E., 1971); Machado, *Poesías completas* (Buenos Aires, 1959); Jiménez, *Tercera antología poética* (Madrid, 1957).

99   Fernando Pessoa, "Maritime Ode," translated and used by permission of Edwin Honig.

100   José Martí, "Two Countries"; translated and used by permission of William Ferguson.

103   Trotsky, vol. 1, *Literatura y revolución*, and vol. 2, *Otros escritos sobre la literatura y el arte* (Paris, 1969). The first two quotations are from vol. 2; the rest from vol. 1.

110–112 Marcel Duchamp, *Étant Donnés: 1. La Chute d'Eau; 2. Le Gaz d'Eclairage* (1946–1966), Assemblage, Philadelphia Museum of Fine Arts.

113   Arthur Rimbaud, "Alchimie du verbe," *Une Saison en Enfer* (1873); "Lettre du voyant" (letter to Paul Demeny, May 15, 1871), *Oeuvres complètes,* ed. Roland de Renéville et Jules Mouquet (Paris, Bibliothèque de la Pléiade, 1946).

113–114 Mallarmé, *Un coup de dés* (Paris, 1897).

117   Baudelaire, *Mon coeur mis à nu* (1862–1864).

119   Hugh Kenner, *The Pound Era* (Berkeley, University of California, 1971); the interview (with D. C. Bridson) appeared in *New Directions* in 1961.

121   T. S. Eliot, "The Metaphysical Poets" (1921), in *Selected Essays* (New York, Harcourt, Brace, 1932).

126   See Roger Shattuck, *The Banquet Years* (New York, Vantage, 1955).

133   James J. Y. Liu, *The Art of Chinese Poetry* (Chicago, University of Chicago Press, 1962).

140   Pound, *Canto* 80; *Pisan Cantos*, 74. *The ABC of Reading* (New York, New Directions).

142   Thomas Ernest Hulme, "Romanticism and Classicism," *Speculations: Essays on Humanism and the Philosophy of Art* (London, Routledge and Kegan Paul, 1924).

145   Eliot, "Dante" (1929), in *Selected Essays*.

157   Paz, "Horas situadas de Jorge Guillén," *Puertas al campo* (2nd ed., Barcelona, Seix Barral, 1972).

163   *Alternating Current*, trans. Helen D. Lane (New York, Viking, 1973); *Conjunctions and Disjunctions*, trans. Helen D. Lane (New York, Viking, 1973); Rita Guibert, *Seven Voices* (New York, Knopf, 1973).

166   Daniel Bell, "The Post-Industrial Society: The Evolution of an Idea," *Survey*, numbers 78 and 79, 1971.

167   In *Alternating Current* I described the differences between revolution, revolt, and rebellion. The classic example of "revolu-

tion'' is still the French Revolution, and I do not know whether it is legitimate to apply this word to the changes which have taken place in Russia, China, and elsewhere, profound and decisive though they may have been. I use the word ''revolt'' to refer to the uprisings and liberation movements of the Third World and Latin America (the latter, strictly speaking, does not belong to the Third World), and ''rebellion'' for the protest movements of ethnic minorities, women's liberation, student and other groups, in industrialized societies.